Lyndey and Blair's
Taste of Greece

A mother and son travel through the Peloponnese

Lyndey and Blair's Taste of Greece

A mother and son travel through the Peloponnese

Lyndey Milan

For Blair

*This was to be your dream
and without you it could
not have been mine.*

A Peloponnese dream 10 ~ Map 14 ~
Athens and Corinth 16 ~ Nemea, Old Corinth and
Vivari Beach 40 ~ Karathona and Nafplio 70 ~
Monemvasia and Kythira 102 ~ Kalogria, Stoupa
and Inner Mani 126 ~ Kalamata, Messene and Outer
Mani 154 ~ Mercouri and Olympia 184 ~
Glossary 212 ~ Useful information and Bibliography 216 ~ Index 218 ~
Acknowledgements 222

A Peloponnese dream

IN SEPTEMBER 2010, my son Blair and I made the road trip of a lifetime around the Peloponnese peninsula in Greece to film the television series, *Lyndey & Blair's Taste of Greece*. This was to be a series unlike any other. Though filmed in a popular location, Greece, it focused on an area off the beaten track, the Peloponnese. There would be glorious scenery but not of the Greek Islands. There would be food, wine and travel but also more: exploration of the archaeology, myths and legends of ancient Greece. And there would be engagement with local characters met along the way.

Not to mention the magic of a unique mother–son relationship. In Blair's own words, 'Travelling and shooting a television program with your mother is a little out of the ordinary! ... The beauty of a mother–son relationship on camera is that you can't fake it or replicate it; all the complexities have been built up over 29 years.'

The television series aired on SBS One in Australia in 2011 to great critical acclaim and is having the same success in the UK and New Zealand with broadcast to follow on a variety of channels across Europe and Asia.

As an actor, Blair had worked hard, hoping for his 'big break' and international fame and it seems it

finally arrived. This is especially poignant because in the very early hours of 17 April, 2011, Blair passed away from acute myeloid leukaemia, only 3 days after diagnosis, and before the series aired. He was an extraordinary 29 year-old who lived life to the full and made a conscious decision to be happy every single day of his life. He brought joy into the lives of all he met and always signed off with the words, 'Good times!'

This book was to be *our* book: my eighth but his first, a joyful collaboration between mother and son. This was not to be, but I trust that the end result gives even greater depth to our journey than did the television series. The photos and memories are all there, as are the recipes we cooked or ate in Greece, Blair's cocktails inspired by his night clubbing in Athens, and snippets about the archaeological sites we visited on our trip.

The success of the show is made all the more special because the series evolved as a matter of chance. My partner, John, and I had been discussing television shows with an old friend and colleague who is of Greek descent. John has a Master of Arts in Classics from the University of Cambridge and has a great love of archaeology and history, especially that of Greece. As the wine flowed, we talked about the type of television show we would like to watch and how wonderful it would be to create a new genre in an era dominated by 'reality' shows. And the next morning in the clear light of day, it still seemed just as good an idea. I was no longer tied down by any work contracts, my friend was keen to be co-host and so our determination to make a series was born. We met with television networks and Greek government representatives in Australia, then John and I engaged a series producer and headed off to Greece to meet with government officials there.

Fast forward to 6 weeks prior to shooting: the trip was planned, crew engaged, permits sought, but my co-host had to withdraw. We were committed to the series and looked at the options. Should I go it alone, find another Greek–Australian personality or find a co-host in Greece? Hearing our dilemma, John's best friend said, 'The answer is obvious — take Blair.' What inspiration and, as it turns out, what a blessing!

Blair leapt at the chance and threw himself into the preparations in his characteristic wholehearted fashion. Suddenly, the style of the show morphed as, with a fit and active young co-host, an element of adventure entered the equation. No longer was it a Greek–Australian showing his friend his homeland, it was a mother and son duo discovering the country together, each with their own interests.

I had been to Greece a few times over many years but Blair had only ever been to Corfu. However,

he had links with Greece, having starred in Greek philosophy plays, The Philosophy of Freedom in 2005 and The Philosophy of Love in 2006, both for the Greek Festival of Sydney. It just seemed so right to be going together. And so it was. Blair was a joy on the road — enthusiastic, hardworking and uncomplaining over the long, arduous hours of shooting, great mates with the crew and the first to buy the bus driver a drink. Best of all he took a shine to the history and archaeology of this ancient land, asking John question after question, and lapping up the knowledge. He was my perfect foil.

I will never forget his bold bungy jump over the spectacular Corinth Canal — or my nervousness as I watched. Blair embraced all the flavours of Greece, relishing all the new experiences; except that is, for the tripe soup. Even garlic, vinegar and chilli flakes couldn't make that work for him!

So it's all here in this book. The stories, the anecdotes and history. The recipes old and new and those which are my take on Greek food. Food in Greece is entirely seasonal so whatever ingredients you have to hand, I hope this book will help you cook with a Greek heart and so create your own sun-kissed dishes. Greek may be a cuisine a little forgotten in the modern world but with its vibrant flavours it is one well worth rediscovering. May this book help you to do so — and also remember a wonderful young man.

We owe the aphorism 'Whom the gods love die young' to the Roman playwright, Plautus, but, like many Roman authors, Plautus was distilling an earlier Greek idea. The fifth-century historian, Herodotus, describes the early deaths of two young men, Cleobis and Biton. Their mother was a priestess of Hera and she was keen to attend a festival in honour of the goddess. However, the oxen used to draw her carriage were unavailable, so these stalwart youths put themselves to the yoke and drew the carriage for 'forty-five furlongs [8.3 kilometres] to the temple of Hera' where 'they made a most excellent end of their lives', presumably dying from exhaustion. 'And thus,' concludes Herodotus, 'the gods showed by these men how it was better for a man to die than to live.'

So we have the concept that when we have reached perfection, we can leave this life.

Vale Blair.

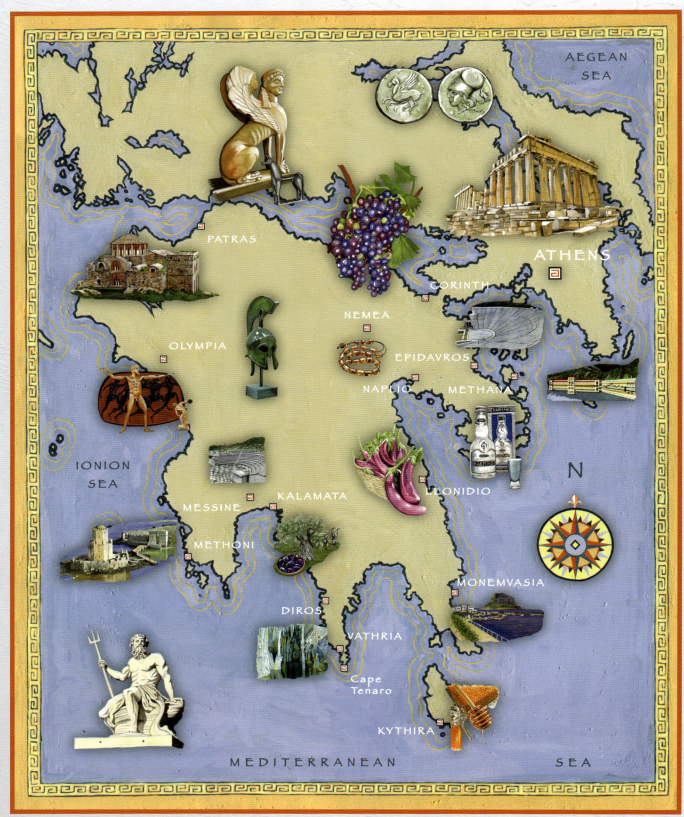

Mikra garídia kai psaría tiganíta ~ Pàtsas ~
Pastítsio ~ Hiríno keftédes may oúzo ~ Mícra
octapódia marinátos ~ Risóto may kapsalismeni
kalambóki, kolokitha, tiri katsíkiou kai safráni
~ Arní keftédes ~ Revithókeftedes me róka
saláta kai stafídes ~ Ellinikí keík me tíri me ksíra
stafídes ~ Ellinkó pagató may yohórti kai méli me
zésti sirópi apó sikó glykó

Chapter 1
Athens and Corinth

Athens is both modern and ancient:

a bustling city full of monuments. It oozes history and culture. As a first timer, Blair was excited to be there and keen to climb the Acropolis, perched high above the city, the first democratic centre of the ancient world. But first I had to take him to the Agora meat market for a taste of their famous tripe soup. Despite Blair having been brought up to try everything, this was not a hit, so we headed off to the long-established Stani Patisserie where a plate of their stunning Greek yoghurt with honey and walnuts and an icy frappé set us up for our whirlwind day in Athens.

Not only did we visit the Acropolis museum, but we got to see inside an apartment, visiting a friend, George, who is the son of a very well-known artist, Nikos Kypraios. Here we sipped on sweet Samos wine before visiting Brettos distillery, one of the oldest bars in the city and famous for serving 642 different drinks. Blair's mania for cocktails sent him into the night in a quest for new and interesting Greek cocktails, while I learned a modern spin on Greek food, cooking at Kuzina Restaurant with owner and chef, Aris Tsanaklidis.

Despite the late night, the next day we were on our way, and the first stop was the Corinth Canal that connects the Gulf of Corinth with the Saronic Gulf. We caught a boat along the six kilometre length of the canal and looked up at the drop of 79 metres. I was none too pleased when I learned that Blair has arranged a bungy jump, but conveniently not mentioned it to me!

Fried small prawns and baby fish

Mikra garídia kai psaría tiganíta

Marida are little fish, a bit like large whitebait; they are deep-fried as a meze, along with school prawns. Enjoyed all over Greece, they are often accompanied by ouzo. They were a surprise treat when Blair and I ordered ouzo on the boat on the Corinth Canal.

Pour plenty of oil into a medium heavy-based saucepan and place over a medium–high heat.

Place the flour in a small plastic bag and season it well with salt and freshly ground black pepper. Add the prawns and fish, in batches if necessary, then twist the top of the bag to close. Shake until they are coated with the seasoned flour.

Test the heat of the oil with a wooden implement or tip of a prawn to see if bubbles appear. Shake the prawns and fish to remove excess flour, then cook, in batches if necessary, for 1–2 minutes, or until the prawns are pink and the fish is opaque and both are crisp. Drain well on paper towels. Serve immediately with lemon wedges.

Lyndey's note *If the prawns are small enough, they can be eaten whole, leaving the shells and heads on. If you prefer, you can remove the heads but please leave the shells and tails on — they are amazingly crisp when deep-fried.*

SERVES 4 as part of a meze
Preparation and cooking time 10 minutes

extra-virgin olive oil for deep-frying
plain flour, for dusting
250 g small raw prawns (shrimp) (see Lyndey's note)
200 g whitebait or other small fish
lemon wedges to serve

Tripe soup
Patsas

How could I ever forget Blair's reaction to tripe soup? He was not a fan. My own initial reaction was more positive — the first time I tried it was at 3 a.m. after a night out and it was just perfect for that hour. It is one of the classics of traditional Greek cuisine and a fixture at the Agora (meat market) in Athens. I had to create my version for you.

If time allows, make the skordóstoumbi several hours ahead of time or overnight to steep the flavours. Combine the vinegar and garlic, cover and stand at room temperature.

To make the soup, wash the tripe well, place it in a large saucepan, cover with cold water, and add the lemon juice. Place the saucepan over a medium heat and bring slowly to the boil. Reduce the heat to low and simmer, uncovered, for 5 minutes. Drain, rinse the tripe well under cold water and cool it slightly. Cut the blanched tripe into fine strips. Rinse out the saucepan.

Return the tripe to the clean saucepan and add the stock. Bring it slowly to the boil, reduce the heat to low and simmer for 5 minutes. Remove any scum that rises. Add the garlic, onion, peppercorns, bay leaf, thyme and salt. Simmer for 1 hour, or until the tripe is very tender.

To serve, add the parsley, season to taste with salt and freshly ground black pepper and simmer for a further 1 minute. Serve with the Skordóstoumbi and dried chilli flakes — each person can add as much of each as they like.

Lyndey's note Every table at the restaurant at which we ate tripe soup — Papandreou's Agora Tavern — had a bowl of skordóstoumbi. There the garlic was kept whole but I prefer to slice it as it infuses the flavours better. Chilli flakes are an optional addition. Blair loaded his soup with chilli flakes to make it more palatable!

SERVES 4
Preparation and cooking time
1¼–1¾ hours

500 g honeycomb tripe
juice of 1 lemon
2 litres good-quality chicken stock
3 large garlic cloves, peeled and smashed
1 onion, chopped
½ teaspoon whole black peppercorns
1 bay leaf
5 thyme sprigs
2 teaspoons sea salt flakes, or to taste
1 small handful flat-leaf parsley
dried chilli flakes to serve (optional)

Skordóstoumbi
¾ cup red wine vinegar
3 garlic cloves, peeled and very finely sliced

Pastitsio

Pastitsio

The meat market was full of whole carcasses, poultry, offal and lots and lots of lamb. The visit made me want to cook for myself and this is one of the famous traditional dishes of Greek cuisine though outside Greece it is a little less well known than its relative, moussaka.

SERVES 8–10
Preparation and cooking time
2 hours

Heat a large, deep frying pan over a medium heat and crumble in half of the minced lamb. Cook the lamb until it is well browned and any liquid has evaporated, breaking up any lumps with a fork. Remove the first batch, reheat the frying pan and cook the remaining lamb, then remove from the pan.

Reheat the frying pan, add the oil, then the onion and garlic. Cook for 2 minutes over a medium heat, add the tomato paste, and cook, stirring, for 1 minute. Add the wine, tomato purée and the browned mince and stir well before adding the nutmeg, sugar, salt, bay leaves and cloves. Bring to the boil, reduce the heat to low and simmer for 30–40 minutes, adding a little water if needed. Once the sauce is cooked, remove the cloves.

Meanwhile, cook the macaroni in a large saucepan of boiling salted water for 8–10 minutes, or until just tender (check the packet instructions). Drain and set aside to cool slightly. Mix with the kefalotyri and egg.

To make the cheese sauce, melt the butter in a small saucepan over a medium–low heat until it froths. Add the flour and stir for 2 minutes. Gradually pour in the milk, whisking constantly until the mixture comes to the boil and is thick and smooth. Remove from the heat and cool slightly. Add the eggs, kefalotyri and nutmeg and whisk to combine. Season to taste with salt and freshly ground black pepper.

Preheat the oven to 180°C (160°C fan-forced). Grease a deep roasting tin or baking dish with melted butter or oil. Place half of the macaroni over the base of the dish. Spoon half of the meat sauce over the pasta. Repeat the layer of pasta and meat sauce. Pour the cheese sauce over the top, then smooth the surface. Sprinkle with breadcrumbs and bake for 50 minutes. Sprinkle with the extra kefalotyri and bake for a further 20–30 minutes, or until golden. Allow to stand for 5 minutes before serving.

Lyndey's note *I used long tubes of macaroni, much like the Italian bucatini pasta (hollow spaghetti), though short macaroni works too. What is important is to use pasta with holes through it so it can absorb the cheese sauce.*

1 kg minced lamb
2 tablespoons extra-virgin olive oil
1 brown onion, chopped
3 garlic cloves, crushed
2 tablespoons tomato paste
½ cup red wine
3 cups tomato purée
½ teaspoon ground nutmeg
2 teaspoons sugar
2 teaspoons salt
2 bay leaves
4 cloves
500 g macaroni (see Lyndey's note)
½ cup grated kefalotyri or pecorino
1 egg, lightly beaten
1½ cups fresh breadcrumbs
1 cup grated kefalotyri or pecorino, extra

Cheese sauce
90 g butter
⅓ cup plain flour
1 litre milk
4 eggs, lightly beaten
½ cup grated kefalotyri or pecorino
½ teaspoon ground nutmeg

Athens after dark

Blair was a flair bartender at times during his university studies and in acting breaks. He kept a little book in which he wrote up classic and other cocktails. He loved the nightclub scene in Athens when he visited the Gazi area with George Kypraios. These Greek-inspired cocktails commemorate that.

All recipes make one cocktail.

Ginger and lime daiquiri *Tzínzer kai laim dákiri*

SERVES 1 Preparation time 5 minutes

Cut 1 lime into eighths and muddle the wedges with 1 teaspoon warm honey in a highball glass. Add 45 ml vodka, mix well, then top up with ginger beer to taste.

Under the Hellenic sun *Káto apó ton Ellinikó ílio*

SERVES 1 Preparation time 5 minutes

Fill a highball glass with ice, add 15 ml ouzo and 30 ml peach schnapps and top with half orange juice and half soda water. Garnish with an orange wedge.

Red rock *Kókkinos vráchos*

SERVES 1 Preparation time 5 minutes

Mix 30 ml citron vodka, 30 ml Cointreau, 15 ml lime juice and a splash of blood orange juice in a cocktail glass. Top with sparkling wine or soda water. Serve with a lime wedge on the side.

Blood of Hercules *Emeh tón Iráklies*

SERVES 1 Preparation time 5 minutes

Combine 40 ml Agiorgitiko or dry red wine, 20 ml tequila, 60 ml pomegranate juice and 15 ml honey syrup (1 part honey: 1 part water) in a highball glass. Add ice and float pomegranate seeds over the top.

Long sparkling ouzo *Makrí oúzo afródis*

SERVES 1 Preparation time 5 minutes

Fill a highball glass with ice, add 45 ml ouzo and 15 ml lime juice. Drink as it is for a stronger cocktail or top with soda water and serve with a mint sprig.

Sparkling watermelon with ouzo foam
H' Afródis karpóuzi may ton afró oúzo

SERVES 1 Preparation time 5 minutes

Place 60 g watermelon flesh, 20 ml ouzo, 15 ml lime juice and some ice in a blender and blend until smooth. Strain into a martini glass and top with sparkling wine.

From left: Sparkling watermelon with ouzo foam, Under the Hellenic sun, Ginger and lime daiquiri, Long sparkling ouzo, Red rock, Blood of Hercules.

Braised pork keftedes flavoured with ouzo

Hirino keftedes may ouzo

Drinking ouzo led me to think about cooking with ouzo and how that might subtly change flavours. It works a treat in these tender meatballs.

Place the bread in a small bowl and pour over enough water to just cover it. Soak for 5 minutes.

Heat 1 tablespoon of the oil a small frying pan, add the onion and cook over a low heat to soften but not colour it. Add the garlic, cook for a further 30 seconds and then remove the pan from the heat.

Use your hand to squeeze any excess water from the bread. Combine the pork, soaked bread, cooked onion and garlic, ouzo, rigani and salt and mix well. Shape into small balls and gently flatten and taper the ends — you should get about 30 balls. Place the keftedes on a tray and refrigerate for 15 minutes.

Meanwhile, heat the remaining 1 tablespoon oil in a large, deep frying pan over a medium heat. Add the extra onion and cook, stirring, for 1 minute, then add the tomato purée and stock. Bring the liquid to the boil, then reduce the heat and simmer for 5 minutes.

To finish the keftedes, heat the extra oil in a large frying pan over a medium heat. Working in two batches, dust the keftedes lightly with flour and fry for 2–3 minutes, turning to brown them all over. Using tongs, transfer the keftedes from the frying pan to the simmering tomato sauce. Simmer gently in the sauce until cooked through and the sauce has thickened slightly. Sprinkle with the parsley to serve.

> SERVES 4
> Preparation and cooking time
> 40 minutes

2 slices white bread, crusts removed
2 tablespoons extra-virgin olive oil
1 small onion, finely chopped
2 large garlic cloves, crushed
500 g minced pork
¼ cup ouzo or white wine or water
1 tablespoon rigani
2 teaspoons sea salt flakes
1 onion, extra, finely chopped
3 cups tomato purée
2 cups beef stock
¼ cup extra-virgin olive oil, extra
plain flour for dusting
flat-leaf parsley to serve

OCTOPUS AND SQUID

Octopus and squid were popular in classical times as a source of food but they were also studied in classical zoology. Both are cephalopods, so named because their tentacles grow directly from their heads. They were admired for their ability to change colour for camouflage and eject ink to screen themselves from predators. However, it was their interesting form and the curling tentacles that were frequently depicted in Ancient Greek art. The writer Athenaios praised their 'wonderful curls'.

The octopus has eight tentacles instead of the squid's ten and its popularity in ancient times is evident from the way it was depicted on classical Greek vases, many of which survive today.

Octopus and squid can be cooked in the same way. First tenderise it by bashing against the rocks — forty times according to Greek fishermen. Freezing also works as a method of tenderising and in Greece frozen cephalopods are served out of season. They can be braised, fried, stuffed and grilled and, in some areas of Greece, you see them hung out to dry. They are perennially popular, especially as they are allowed during the abstinence of Lent.

Baby octopus marinated in honey

Mícra octapódia marinátos

After enjoying some modern Greek food at the Kuzina Restaurant in Athens I wanted to create my own modern Greek dishes, using Greek flavours but in a more modern way as with these baby octopus. Serve them with Greek salad or as part of a meze. (Picture on page 84.)

To clean each octopus, use a small sharp knife and remove the head from the tentacles. Either discard the head or slit it open and remove the insides, then slice it in half. Remove the beak from the tentacles by pushing your index finger into the centre of the body. Rinse the octopus thoroughly then pat dry with paper towels.

Combine the octopus with the vinegar, honey and oil. Marinate for 1 hour in the refrigerator.

To cook the octopus, preheat a barbecue flat plate or chargrill plate to very hot. Use tongs to remove the octopus from the marinade, shaking off the excess so the octopus is not too wet as it hits the barbecue plate. Cook the octopus in small batches for 2—3 minutes, turning once, and then remove to a serving plate. Do not crowd the barbecue plate or the octopus will stew.

| SERVES 4—6
Preparation and cooking time
25 minutes + 1 hour marinating

1 kg baby octopus
¼ cup red wine vinegar
¼ cup honey
¼ cup extra-virgin olive oil

Risotto with charred corn, pumpkin, goat's cheese and saffron

Risóto may kapsalismeni kalambóki, kolokitha, tiri katsikiou kai safráni

Aris from the contemporary Kuzina restaurant in Athens showed me that not all Greek food is traditional. As he cooks to order, he does some pre-preparation with the rice and cooks one portion at a time. Here his recipe is quadrupled to make enough for four people.

SERVES 4
Preparation and cooking time
30 minutes

Heat 2 cups of the stock in a medium saucepan on the stove or in a container in the microwave until hot.

Infuse the saffron in 1 tablespoon warm water.

Par-cook the rice by combining the rice, a pinch of salt and the wine in a medium saucepan over a medium–high heat. Evaporate off the wine, and then add the hot stock. Boil for 4 minutes, or until the liquid has evaporated. Remove the pan from the heat and spread the rice out on a baking tray to cool quickly. Set the rice aside.

Place a large heavy-based saucepan over a high heat and heat until the saucepan is hot. Add the corn kernels to the saucepan and cook for 5 minutes, stirring occasionally, or until the corn smells toasted, chars and begins to pop. Add the oil, stir to coat the corn kernels, then add the pumpkin, onion and cooled rice and mix well.

Add the remaining cold stock, softened saffron and sultanas and season well with salt and freshly ground black pepper. Reduce the heat and cook, uncovered, for 10 minutes, or until the liquid is absorbed and the rice and vegetables are tender.

Stir in the parmesan, soft curd cheese, half of the myzithra cheese and the butter. Taste, and if using ricotta, which doesn't have the acid of a goat's cheese, add lemon juice to taste. Serve topped with the remaining myzithra cheese.

Lyndey's note *During a fasting period, such as Lent, vegetable stock is used. Aris uses hot stock for the first cooking of the rice and cold for the second so that the rice doesn't overcook.*

- 1.5 litres chicken or vegetable stock (see Lyndey's note)
- good pinch of saffron threads
- 2 cups vialone nano or arborio rice
- ½ cup white wine
- 2–3 fresh corn cobs, kernels removed (about 230 g kernels)
- 1 tablespoon extra-virgin olive oil
- 300 g pumpkin, diced into 1 cm pieces
- 1 small red onion, chopped
- 1 cup sultanas
- ⅓ cup grated parmesan
- 120 g soft curd cheese, such as ksinotiri from Crete, goat's curd or smooth ricotta
- ¼ cup finely grated myzithra cheese or parmesan
- 60 g butter
- about 1 tablespoon lemon juice (optional)

Lamb keftedes
Arni keftédes

While keftedes are a staple of Greek cuisine, here they are given a more modern twist. (Picture on page 85.)

Mix together the lamb, salt, cumin, cinnamon, egg, breadcrumbs and mint in a large bowl. Take approximately 1 tablespoon of the mixture and shape into small round meatballs. Lay the keftedes in a single layer on a tray and refrigerate while you prepare the eggplant sauce.

To make the eggplant sauce, cut the eggplants into large cubes, sprinkle with the salt and stand for 10 minutes. Rinse the eggplant and then pat it dry with a clean tea towel. Heat 1 tablespoon of the oil in a large frying pan over a medium heat. Cook the eggplant in two or three batches, adding more oil as needed. Return all the eggplant to the frying pan, add the tomatoes, water, cumin, cinnamon and sugar. Simmer, uncovered, stirring often until the eggplant is tender, but still holding its shape — the eggplant mixture should be slightly thick. Cool slightly then stir in the parsley.

To serve, brush the keftedes with olive oil, preheat a large frying pan and cook the keftedes, in batches if necessary, for 5–8 minutes, shaking the pan and rolling the keftedes, so they are well browned and cooked through.

While the keftedes are cooking, process the yoghurt and mint leaves to make a thin sauce. Pat the vine leaves dry and deep-fry in a little olive if you wish. Warm or toast the pita bread and serve it with the vine leaves and minted yoghurt alongside the keftedes and eggplant sauce.

MAKES about 25. Serve as part of a meze
Preparation and cooking time
40 minutes

500 g minced lamb
1½ teaspoons sea salt flakes, or to taste
1 teaspoon ground cumin
½ teaspoon ground cinnamon
1 egg, lightly beaten
⅓ cup fresh breadcrumbs
¼ cup finely chopped mint leaves
olive oil for brushing

Eggplant sauce
2 large eggplants (aubergines)
1 tablespoon salt
¼ cup extra-virgin olive oil
2 garlic cloves, crushed
400 g can diced tomatoes
1 cup water
1 teaspoon ground cumin
½ teaspoon ground cinnamon
½ teaspoon sugar
1 cup flat-leaf parsley, roughly chopped

To serve
½ cup Greek-style natural yoghurt
½ cup mint leaves
vine leaves
extra-virgin olive oil for deep-frying (optional)
Greek pita, toasted

Chickpea fritters with a salad of rocket and raisins

Revithókeftedes me róka saláta kai stafídes

Greeks do not eat vast quantities of meat, except perhaps at Easter. They make good use of everything available and eat a lot of salad, vegetables, beans and pulses. Using canned chickpeas saves a lot of time.

Heat the oil in a small frying pan, add the onion and cook over a low heat to soften but not colour it.

Drain and rinse the chickpeas and remove the skins if you prefer (see Lyndey's note). Mash half of the chickpeas, leaving the remaining chickpeas whole.

To make the fritters, gently mix together the onion, chickpeas, potato, egg, flour, dill, parsley and salt. Take approximately 3 level tablespoons of the mixture and shape into patties. Refrigerate for 15 minutes before cooking.

To cook the fritters, heat the oil in a large frying pan over a medium–high heat and cook the fritters in batches for 2–3 minutes on each side, or until golden and cooked through. Reduce the heat to medium if they are cooking too quickly.

To make the rocket and raisin salad, mix together the muscatels, rocket and a little of the oil. Serve the salad with the chickpea fritters.

Lyndey's note *This is a nifty way to remove the skin from chickpeas. Place the drained chickpeas in a large bowl of water. Working under the water, gently roll the chickpeas around your palms and the skins will slip away. Skim off the skins before you drain the chickpeas.*

SERVES 4
Preparation and cooking time
30 minutes + 15 minutes refrigeration

2 teaspoons extra-virgin olive oil
1 small red onion, finely chopped
400 g can chickpeas
1 large potato, boiled, peeled and mashed
1 egg, lightly beaten
½ cup plain flour
1 cup dill, chopped
2 tablespoons chopped flat-leaf parsley
1½ teaspoons sea salt flakes, or to taste
½ cup extra-virgin olive oil for frying

Rocket and raisin salad
½ cup muscatels or raisins, steeped in a little sweet wine
1 bunch rocket (arugula)
extra-virgin olive oil

Cheesecake with muscatels

Tziskeiik me tiri may ksira stafides

We really enjoyed the nectar sweet Samos wine when we drank it in Athens, so thought it would be perfect to plump up some muscatels to go with a cheesecake, inspired by what we saw at Stani Patisserie.

Warm the wine slightly, taking care not to boil it. Soak the muscatels in the wine, preferably overnight.

Preheat the oven to 160°C (140°C fan-forced). Grease and line the base and side of a 20 cm springform tin with baking paper.

Use an electric beater to beat the cream cheese in a large bowl until smooth. Add the goat's curd, brown sugar and vanilla essence, then beat well. Add the eggs, one at a time, beating well after each addition. Stir in the semolina and cinnamon.

Pour the mixture into the tin and bake for 40–50 minutes, or until it is just set in centre. Turn the oven off and leave the cheesecake to cool in the oven with the door slightly ajar.

Dust the cheesecake with a generous amount of icing sugar, and serve with the muscatels and soaking wine.

Lyndey's note *This cheesecake may crack, but I think that's part of its simple charm — you'll find its fabulous flavour and texture wins you over. I like to cook it and serve it at room temperature on the day it is made.*

SERVES 6
Preparation and cooking time
1 hour 5 minutes + overnight marinating

100 ml Samos liqueur wine or other sweet Muscat-style wine
200 g muscatels left on the stalk
500 g cream cheese, at room temperature
200 g goat's curd
¾ cup soft brown sugar
1 teaspoon vanilla essence
4 eggs
¼ cup fine semolina
1 teaspoon ground cinnamon
icing sugar to serve

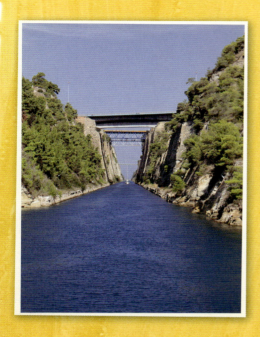

▨▨▨▨▨ ▨▨▨▨▨

CORINTH CANAL/ZULU BUNGY

The spectacular Corinth Canal is a feat of engineering — a man-made canal that connects the Gulf of Corinth with the Saronic Gulf. In ancient times it was much desired as a shortcut for transport vessels. It was Emperor Nero who struck the first blow with a golden pickaxe just before he was assassinated in AD 68, which led to the project being abandoned. It stagnated until the 1870s and was eventually completed in 1893. Built at sea level, it is 6 kilometres long, 8 metres deep and carved out 80 metres below the land's surface. In earlier times boats were rolled on logs from one waterway to another but now it saves smaller vessels some 700 kilometres by not having to circumnavigate the Peloponnese.

It was only when we stopped to admire the canal and ponder its history that Blair dropped his bombshell — he was going to bungy jump from the top. I was not happy but when I met the wonderful owners, Andy and Sotiris, heard about their great track record and experience and saw others try it, I felt slightly calmer but still oh so anxious, as the camera showed. When Blair made that amazing jump, he was so exhilarated that I felt a mixture of relief, excitement and pride. I'm so glad that Blair lived life to the full.

▨▨▨▨▨ ▨▨▨▨▨

Greek yoghurt and honey ice cream with a warm syrupy dried fig spoon sweet

Ellinkó pagató may yohórti kai méli me zesti sirópi apó sikó glykó

Greek yoghurt and honey is eaten for breakfast by tourists or for dessert by Greeks and is something we enjoyed everywhere we went. So what a great idea to make it into ice cream with an easier version of the classic Greek spoon sweet (a sweet jam served by the spoonful).

SERVES 4
Preparation and cooking time
45 minutes + freezing time

Place the sugar and water in a small saucepan and stir over a low heat to dissolve the sugar. Increase the heat to medium and simmer gently for 3 minutes. Cool the syrup to room temperature.

Combine the yoghurt, cream, honey, orange zest and juice. Add the cooled syrup to the yoghurt mixture.

Pour the mixture into a large shallow cake tin and freeze until frozen at the edges. Beat with electric beaters until smooth and creamy. Repeat the freezing and beating process twice more, then pour the mixture into a smaller, deeper cake tin (to help give you good-sized scoops of ice cream) and freeze for several hours, or until firm.

While the ice cream freezes, make the dried fig spoon sweet. Place the honey, orange and lemon juice and cinnamon stick in a small saucepan and cook over a medium heat until the mixture boils. Reduce the heat to low, add the figs and simmer for about 20 minutes, or until the mixture is syrupy. Stand at room temperature until you are ready to serve.

Serve the warm syrup over the scoops of ice cream.

½ cup sugar
½ cup water
500 g Greek-style natural yoghurt
1 cup cream
½ cup honey
grated zest and juice of 1 small orange

Dried fig spoon sweet
½ cup honey
¾ cup orange juice
juice of 1 lemon
1 cinnamon stick, broken into thirds
375 g dried figs, cut into quarters

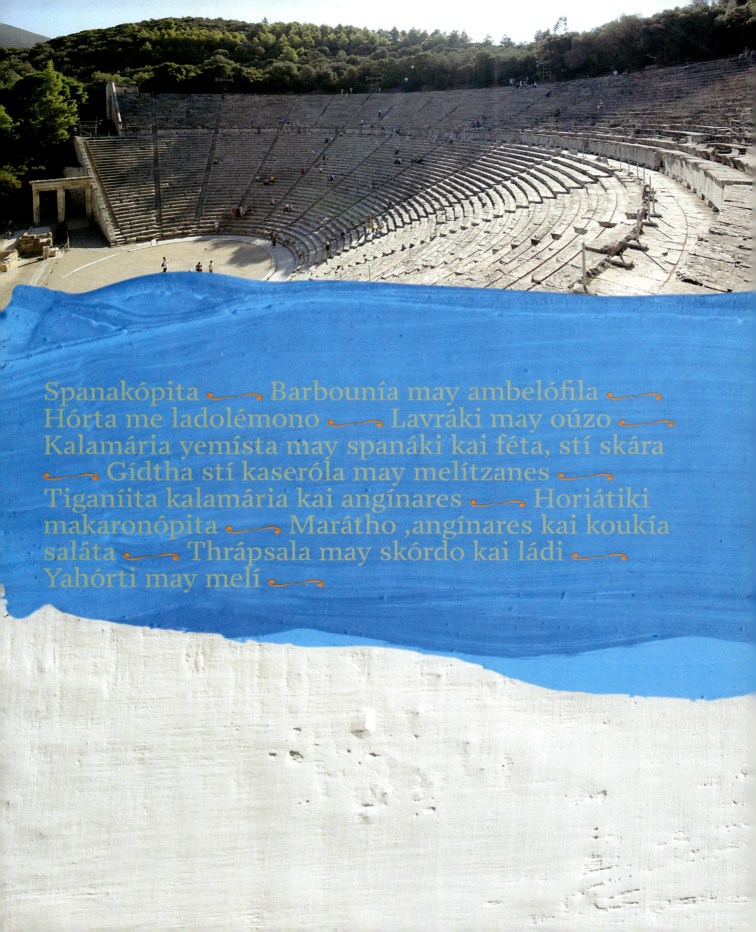

Spanakópita Barbounía may ambelófila
Hórta me ladolémono Lavráki may oúzo
Kalamária yemísta may spanáki kai féta, stí skára
 Gídtha stí kaseróla may melítzanes
Tiganíita kalamária kai angínares Horiátiki
makaronópita Marátho ,angínares kai koukía
saláta Thrápsala may skórdo kai ládi
Yahórti may melí

Chapter 2
Nemea, Old Corinth and Viviari Beach

After  a late night in Athens

I planned a rehydrating visit to the Loutraki thermal spa for Blair. The bathing belles may not have been quite what he had in mind but nonetheless he embraced the experience. We then had lunch at Gemelos Taverna with its rooftop balcony overlooking the fabulous ruins of Ancient Corinth. Afterwards we climbed to the top of the imposing fortress of Acrocorinth. Finally, we were let loose in one of the most famous vineyards in Greece, Gaia, with the charming Yiannis Paraskevopoulos, one of Greece's foremost winemakers. He explained the unique characteristics of the Nemean wine region and introduced us to its indigenous grape, agiorgitiko. Just the thing to accompany this wine proved to be goat with eggplant, carefully prepared by his friend Maria, a chef from the local village.

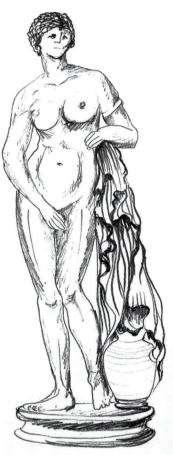

The next morning I was up at dawn to buy produce at the market. Blair was keen for his culture hit of the day and we were blown away by the grandeur of Epidavros, an ancient amphitheatre with the most astonishing acoustics. Of course, we had to put it to the test for ourselves. Blair loved the water and couldn't wait to get into it again, but this time it was the strong smelling sulphurous water of Methana, which didn't go down too well with the crew when we re-boarded the bus. But they were appeased when we cooked them a seafood feast on Drepano beach. Helped by an ouzo or two we relaxed into the sunset.

Silverbeet pie
Spanakópita

Spanakopita is one of the classics of Greek cuisine and is an important part of the Lenten menu. It can be made as a pie (as here) or as small triangles and served as part of a meze. We ate a delicious version at Gemelos Taverna.

If the filo is frozen, remove it from the freezer and place in the refrigerator the day before it is needed. Remove the filo from the refrigerator 30 minutes before starting the recipe.

Finely chop the silverbeet, place in a large colander over a bowl and sprinkle evenly with the salt. Place a heavy weight on top — a large dinner plate topped with a few tins or jars works well — and leave for 1 hour to drain.

Preheat the oven to 200°C (180°C fan-forced). Grease the base and sides of a 25 x 35 cm baking dish with a little oil and line the base with baking paper.

Rinse the silverbeet thoroughly under running water, drain well and squeeze out as much water as possible. Place in a large bowl, add the green onions, dill, mint, feta and eggs and mix well. Season with salt and freshly ground black pepper, remembering that feta is salty and the spinach has been salted.

Dampen a clean tea towel with water. Remove the filo from the packet, unroll carefully, cover with a large piece of baking paper and top with the damp tea towel. To ensure the filo doesn't dry out and tear, each time you remove a sheet, replace the baking paper and tea towel.

Working with one sheet at a time, lay 14 filo sheets into the prepared baking dish, brushing every second sheet with the oil. Top with the silverbeet mixture, spreading it out evenly and pressing with the back of a spoon to pack it tightly. Top with the remaining filo sheets, brushing every second sheet with oil. Brush the top sheet and tuck any excess filo into the baking dish. Using a sharp knife, cut into squares, three-quarters of the way through to the bottom of the tray.

Bake for 50-60 minutes, or until the top of the pie is golden and crisp. Stand for 5 minutes before serving. Cut the squares through to the bottom and use a spatula to carefully remove the pieces. Serve hot or at room temperature.

| SERVES 8
| Preparation and cooking time
| 2 hours

375 g packet filo pastry, about 22 sheets
2–3 bunches (750 g) silverbeet (Swiss chard), stems removed
1 tablespoon salt
1 bunch (300 g) green onions (shallots), trimmed and cut into 5 mm slices
¼ cup finely chopped dill
¼ cup finely chopped mint leaves
200 g feta, crumbled
3 eggs, lightly beaten
¾ cup extra-virgin olive oil

Barbounia wrapped in vine leaves
Barbounia may ambelófila

Barbounia are small red mullet that only take a minute or so on each side to cook. If they are not available, white fish fillets such as whiting or flathead are superb cooked in vine leaves. These are ideal as finger food or part of a meze with ouzo on ice.

Rinse the vine leaves, pat dry with paper towels and lay out flat. Place one fish in the middle of each vine leaf. Fold in the two sides, then roll up and place on a plate, join side down.

Heat the oil in a large frying pan over a medium heat. Add the fish, join side down, and cook for 3 minutes on each side, depending on the size of the fish. You may want to unwrap one to ensure it is cooked through.

Serve immediately with lemon wedges or wild greens.

Lyndey's note *Small vine leaves are ideal for this recipe as they allow the head and tail of the fish to peep out. Alternatively, you could cut large vine leaves in half.*

SERVES 10 as part of a meze
Preparation and cooking time 12 minutes

- 10 small vine leaves (see Lyndey's note)
- 10 barbounia (baby red mullet), cleaned, or whiting or flathead fillets
- ¼ cup extra-virgin olive oil
- lemon wedges or wild greens (page 48) to serve

Wild greens

Horta me ladolémono

Horta literally means greens and in Greece everyone eats wild greens, which appear in the fields after the first autumn rains. They also eat farmed summer horta called vlita in Greek, which is sold in Asian supermarkets under the name amaranth or Chinese greens (en choy) — they are easy to spot as they have a deep red flush on the leaf. Long green-leafed chicory works well too.

Cut the long stems off the amaranth just below the bottom leaves and wash well. If the individual bunches are very big, cut them in half.

Fill a very large saucepan with water, add the amaranth and bring to the boil, uncovered, for 5 minutes, or until soft. Once the amaranth leaves have softened, taste them and see if they need more cooking, as horta is generally cooked for longer than other green vegetables. Remove from the pan and drain.

Place on a serving plate, pour over the oil and serve with the lemon wedges.

Lyndey's note *Vlita, or amaranth, boils down to almost nothing so don't be surprised by the amounts given.*

SERVES 4 as a side dish
Preparation and cooking time
20 minutes

1 kg amaranth leaves
   (see Lyndey's note)
¼ cup olive oil
lemon wedges to serve

Sea bass with ouzo
Lavráki may oúzo

I cooked this meal at Vivari Beach at Drepano — I gathered local ingredients and cooked them on the spot. Sea bass is not available in Australia but barramundi makes a good substitute. If the fish is too large for your pan, cut off the head to enable it to fit.

To make the stuffing, heat the oil in a frying pan over a medium–low heat. Add the leeks and cook, stirring often until the leek is wilted and soft, but not brown. Remove from the heat and allow to cool. Add the dill and lemon zest.

Place the stuffing in the fish cavity.

Heat the oil in a deep frying pan (one with a lid) over a medium–high heat and add the fish. Taking care, immediately pour the ouzo into the frying pan and allow it to bubble up. Add the water, cover with the lid and reduce the heat to low. Simmer gently for 8 minutes, then carefully turn the fish over. Replace the lid and cook for a further 7 minutes, or until the fish is opaque and cooked through.

Transfer the fish to a serving platter and pour over the pan juices to serve.

Lyndey's note To serve as a main course you may want to buy slightly larger fish and cook for a further few minutes.

SERVES 4 as part of a menu
Preparation and cooking time 30 minutes

1 kg whole sea bass or barramundi, cleaned and scaled, head intact
¼ cup extra-virgin olive oil
1 cup ouzo
1 cup water

Leek stuffing
¼ cup olive oil
2 young, thin leeks, cut into 1 cm thick slices
½ bunch dill, chopped
finely grated zest of 1 lemon

Barbecued squid filled with spinach and feta

Kalamária yemísta may spanáki kai feta, stí skára

Every Mediterranean cuisine has its own recipe for stuffed squid — this is the Greek version.

SERVES 4
Preparation and cooking time
30 minutes

To clean each calamari, gently pull on the tentacles to remove them. Cut the tentacles off below the head and discard the head. Remove the clear quill from the body and any dark membrane and discard. Salt your fingers to remove the skin. Cut off the side flaps and finely chop with the tentacles. Reserve. Rinse the calamari well and pat dry with paper towels.

To make the stuffing, blanch the spinach leaves and squeeze dry. Crumble the feta into a small bowl and mash with a fork. Add the spinach, pine nuts, garlic, green onions, oregano, dill, lemon zest and reserved chopped calamari, season well with freshly ground black pepper and stir to mix thoroughly.

Use a piping bag or teaspoon to fill the calamari with the stuffing, taking care not to overstuff the hoods. Use a toothpick on each calamari hood to secure the opening and prevent the filling from escaping.

Preheat a barbecue flat plate or non-stick frying pan to hot. Brush the calamari with a little of the oil and cook the calamari for about 3 minutes on each side, turning them so all sides are browned and the filling is heated through. Drizzle with a little lemon juice and extra-virgin olive oil to serve.

8 small calamari (about 80 g each)
lemon juice to serve
extra-virgin olive oil

Feta and green onion stuffing
2 cups (about 100 g) baby spinach leaves
250 g feta, crumbled
¼ cup pine nuts, toasted
1 garlic clove, crushed
2 green onions (shallots), finely chopped
2 tablespoons oregano leaves, finely chopped
½ cup dill, chopped
finely grated zest of 1 lemon

EPIDAVROS

The imposing theatre of Epidavros was built of limestone in the 4th century BC and can seat up to 15,000 people. It is still sometimes used for performances. Famed for its acoustics, a coin dropped centrestage can be heard in the back seats of the theatre — yet noise from the audience is suppressed.

Like many tourists, Blair and I couldn't resist putting on a little act in the theatre. This was one of our favourite archaeological sites with a magnificent, but at the same time incredibly peaceful setting. Little wonder that the theatre was built as part of the sanctuary of Asclepius, the Greek god of healing.

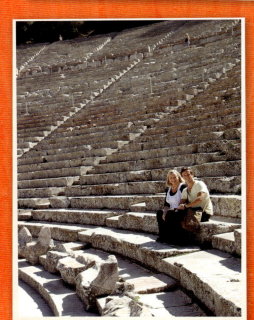

Braised goat with eggplant

Gidtha sti kaseróla may melitzanes

When we cooked this recipe at Gaia, Kyria Maria used a shoulder of nanny goat or, as she referred to it, mother goat, roughly cut into chops (chondra in Greek). She boiled it first for about 45 minutes to tenderise and remove some of the fat. Kyria Maria leaves the boiled goat in the broth to keep it soft until she needs to use it.

In Australia, goat tends to be much younger, smaller and leaner and so it can be cooked for a much briefer time. For a small goat (about 8.5 kilogram whole goat), ask your butcher to cut the leg and shoulder into thick chops. Otherwise just halve the quantities and use either shoulder or leg chops. Lamb can also be substituted.

If using old goat or mutton, rather than young goat, place the chops in a large saucepan and cover with water. Slowly bring to the boil and cook for 45 minutes. Set aside to cool. Remove the fat from the top, reserving the chops and the broth.

Decoratively peel the eggplants by running a vegetable peeler from top to bottom at 3 cm intervals.

Heat 3 tablespoons of the oil in a very large frying pan over a medium–low heat. Add the eggplants and cook, turning frequently, until golden and soft. Set aside.

Heat the remaining oil in a large flameproof casserole dish over a medium heat. Add the goat and cook until the chops are browned. Add the onions, garlic, carrot, cinnamon, cloves, juniper berries, selino, parsley and tomatoes. Pour over the stock (or reserved broth), top with the eggplants and cook for 40–50 minutes, or until tender. Do not stir the eggplants through the mixture.

Lyndey's notes Kyria Maria used two varieties of eggplant: the normal variety, tsakoniki, and a sweeter, seedless variety called flaskes.

Selino is a herb with similar leaves and flavour to celery. Young celery leaves and/or flat-leaf parsley can be substituted.

In the winter ⅓ cup tomato paste can be substituted for the fresh tomatoes.

SERVES 8
Preparation and cooking time
1–1¼ hours

2 kg goat, roughly cut into chops
900 g small eggplants (aubergines) (see Lyndey's notes)
⅓ cup olive oil
2 small red onions, peeled and grated
1–2 garlic cloves, crushed
1 large carrot, cut into fine strips
2 cinnamon sticks
2 cloves
4 juniper berries
½ bunch selino or chopped leaves and stalk of 1 celery stalk (see Lyndey's notes)
¼ cup chopped flat-leaf parsley
6 tomatoes, 4 grated or puréed and 2 chopped) (see Lyndey's notes)
chicken, beef or vegetable stock to cover, or reserved broth

Greek wine

There's so much more to Greek wine than pine-resin flavoured retsina, though this too has its place, especially beside traditional Greek food. It was the ancient Greeks who colonised the Mediterranean with the vine and so are responsible for establishing the French and Italian wine industries.

The wine of Greece has been an important part of the country's culture for more than 3000 years. For much of that time, it has been a highly prized trading commodity, especially around the Mediterranean. When Greece was a Roman province, its wines were often used for Roman banquets when the homegrown product was considered inadequate. During the Byzantine Empire (AD 330–1453) when Constantinople was the centre of the wine trade, and in the years when the Venetians dominated world trade, Greek wine was much sought after. During the rule of the Ottoman Empire (1453–1821) wine production was discouraged, though some of Greece's viticultural resources remained intact.

The tourist boom of the 1960s and rising living standards initiated a demand for bottled wine that was better than retsina and the widely available cheap, bland wines that Greece was producing at the time. The country's entry into the European Union in the mid-1970s made available unprecedented EU subsidies and investment that were channelled into vineyard development and quality wine production. Greek winemakers and viticulturalists began training overseas while working in the vineyards and wineries of Greece to install state-of-the-art technology and knowledge. There was a move towards variety specification and a quality control system similar to those used in France and Italy, as inefficient vineyards and table grapes were replaced by an array of indigenous grape varieties or classic varieties such as chardonnay, cabernet sauvignon and merlot — all part of a move for international recognition.

More recently, vineyards have been planted in cooler sites such as coastal areas and peninsulas where temperatures are moderated by sea breezes and high altitude sites, many between 400 and 800 metres above sea level. Vignerons have been happy with much lower yields than before in pursuit of better quality.

Today, Greek wine presents exciting possibilities for wine lovers. While it is difficult for the classic varieties to compete internationally, there is a growing focus on more than 300 indigenous varieties, with a dozen or so turning heads at home and abroad. These include grapes such as agiorgitiko, athiri, assyrtiko, malagousia, malvasia, moschofilero, robola, roditis, savatiano and xinomavro.

The best varieties have a strong sense of locality. Assyrtiko is the dominant grape of

Santorini and the best examples come from there, although there are some plantings in Northern Greece. Moschofilero is primarily grown on the Mantinia Plateau in the Peloponnese and agiorgitiko is the sole grape planted in the Peloponnese region of Nemea. Xinomavro is found in the warmer north.

Moschofilero is delightful: floral with rose petal aromatics, a savoury minerally palate and lingering, dry acidity while assyrtiko has restrained savoury flavours, gentle viscosity and crisp dry acidity. Both are best unoaked. Xinamavro is a robust, full-bodied red crammed with intense dark berry flavours and powerful tannins balanced by noticeable acidity. Exciting varietals like these are both appealing and the best hope for promoting Greek wines on the international stage.

Most vineyards in Greece are small family holdings of about 1 hectare. However, we were lucky to visit both Mercouri and

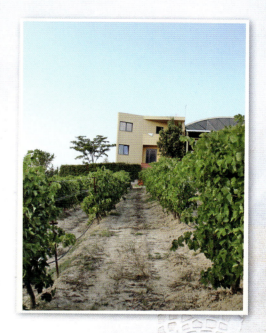

> *Today, Greek wine presents exciting possibilities for wine lovers.*

Gaia Estates. Domaine Mercouri is an old vineyard dating from the late 1800s in the Western Peloponnese. In 1870, the first refosco vines were imported from Friuli, Italy, and planted on the site. With the fourth generation now running the winery, the grape is now locally known as Mercouri.

Agiorgitiko was the discovery of our trip. Also known as St George, because it ripens on St George's Day, it is perhaps the crown jewel in the modern wine industry. It is medium-bodied, best lightly oaked, with redcurrant and blackcurrant flavours, a silky texture and approachable tannins.

There is a synergy between the food and wine of the same soil and these wines work incredibly well with Greek cuisine.

Fried calamari and artichokes

Tiganita kalamária kai anginares

Greek food is entirely seasonal and everything edible is used. Therefore artichokes are used plentifully when they are in season. However, using pre-prepared ones, as I have done here, saves a lot of time.

To clean each calamari, gently pull on the tentacles to remove them. Cut the tentacles off below the head and discard the head. Cut the tentacles into pieces. Remove the clear quill from the body and any dark membrane and discard. Salt your fingers to remove the skin. Cut off the side flaps and slice into strips. Cut open the calamari hoods and slice into strips. Rinse the calamari well and pat dry with paper towels.

Drain the artichokes from the oil, pat dry with paper towels and halve each artichoke.

Place the flour, salt, pepper and rigani in a small plastic bag. Add the calamari and artichokes, in batches if necessary, and shake until they are coated.

Pour oil into a medium heavy-based saucepan to a depth of about 7 cm and place over a medium–high heat. Test the heat of the oil with a wooden implement to see if bubbles appear. Shake the calamari and artichokes to remove any excess flour, then cook, in batches, for about 2 minutes, or until both are crisp. Drain well on paper towels. Fry the parsley in the oil for 20 seconds, or until crisp (stand back as the oil will spit). Drain on paper towels.

Sprinkle the calamari and artichokes with the parsley and serve with wedges of lemon.

Lyndey's note *Rigani is dried Greek oregano and you'll find it in some large delis and spice stores. It is sold in large bags with the herb still on the stalk. It adds a delicious, unmistakeable Greek flavour to dishes. You could substitute dried oregano.*

SERVES 4
Preparation and cooking time
30 minutes

4 large calamari
4–6 artichoke hearts, preserved in oil
⅓ cup plain flour
1 teaspoon salt
1 teaspoon freshly ground black pepper
1 tablespoon rigani (see Lyndey's note)
extra-virgin olive oil for deep-frying
⅓ cup flat-leaf parsley
lemon wedges to serve

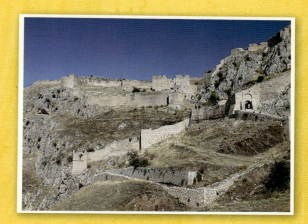

ACROCORINTH

The Acrocorinth was a fortified city set on a steep slope of 575 metres overlooking the ancient city of Corinth. Not only a city in its own right, it was a place of refuge for the people living on the plain below. As we ascended past three consecutive gatehouses, it amazed us that we could see so much evidence of Classical Greek, Byzantine, Norman, Venetian and Turkish occupation. It was here that St Paul visited in the first century AD and railed against the sacred courtesans in the temple of Aphrodite who serviced the men of Corinth. The term 'Corinthian girl' became a synonym for this.

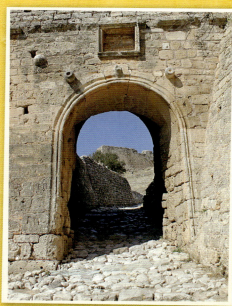

Country-style macaroni pie

Horiátiki makaronópita

Who doesn't love Mac'n'Cheese? Well, this is the Greek version!

SERVES 6–8
Preparation and cooking time
1½ hours

Remove the filo from the refrigerator 30 minutes before starting the recipe.

To make the filling, combine the macaroni, ricotta, feta, haloumi, thyme, parsley, olives, eggs, cream and milk. Season well with salt and freshly ground black pepper. Set aside.

To make the crumb, melt the butter in a small frying pan over a medium heat and add the garlic and breadcrumbs. Cook, stirring often, until the crumbs are golden. Cool slightly, then stir in the thyme and haloumi.

Preheat the oven to 200°C (180°C fan-forced). Lightly grease the base and side of a 6 cm deep, 21 cm springform tin.

Place one sheet of pastry onto the workbench, brush with a little of the oil, and sprinkle with one-fifth of the crumb, then top with a second sheet of filo. Make a further three filo 'sandwiches' — you will end up with one-fifth of the crumbs left over.

Take three of the double sheets of filo and place them over the base and evenly around the side of the tin, arranging them so there are no gaps around the side. Place the filling over the base of the pastry, bring the sides of the filo up, and place the fourth double sheet over the top. Crunch the edges of the filo to seal. Brush the pie with a little oil and sprinkle the remaining crumbs over the top.

Bake for 40–45 minutes, or until the top of the pie is golden and crisp.

Lyndey's note *Thick filo pastry is about 70 per cent thicker than regular filo and the increased sturdiness makes it ideal for larger wraps and pies. It's available chilled (not frozen) from some large delicatessens. To substitute regular filo, use 12 sheets in place of eight. Make four stacks of three, distributing the crumb among all.*

8 sheets of thick filo pastry (see Lyndey's note)
¼ cup extra-virgin olive oil

Macaroni and cheese filling
250 g macaroni, cooked
300 g ricotta, crumbled
100 g feta, crumbled
100 g haloumi, grated
1 tablespoon thyme leaves
¼ cup roughly chopped flat-leaf parsley
½ cup pitted black olives, roughly chopped
2 eggs, lightly beaten
1 cup cream
2 tablespoons milk

Herb and haloumi crumb
60 g butter
2 garlic cloves, crushed
1½ cups fresh breadcrumbs
1 tablespoon thyme leaves
100 g haloumi, grated

Greek salads

There are many more salads popular in Greece than the classic Greek salad. What they have in common is a focus on seasonal vegetables and a liberal dousing of lemon juice and olive oil. These are just three, but the options are endless.

Village salad *Horiátiki saláta*

SERVES 4 Preparation time 15 minutes

Make a simple dressing by whisking together ¼ cup extra-virgin olive oil with 1 tablespoon red wine vinegar or the juice of 1 lemon. Season well with salt and freshly ground black pepper, adding 1 clove of crushed garlic, if you like.

Place 2 chopped Lebanese cucumbers, 1 chopped large green capsicum (pepper), 1 finely sliced red onion, ½ cup kalamata olives and 150 g chopped feta in a salad bowl. Drizzle with the dressing and add fresh oregano leaves or dried rigani, then gently toss and serve.

Marouli salad *Maróuli saláta*

SERVES 4 Preparationt ime 5 minutes + 1 hour soaking

Separate the leaves from 1 large cos lettuce and soak for 1 hour in cool water if you have time. Drain but do not dry completely. Squeeze the leaves between your hands and then finely shred them. Place in a large serving bowl and add 6 finely sliced green onions (shallots) and 2 tablespoons chopped dill.

Combine ⅓ cup extra-virgin olive oil and 1½–2 tablespoons lemon juice in a screw-top jar, and shake well. About 30 minutes before serving, dress the salad and gently toss. Add salt to season the salad and adjust the lemon juice to taste.

Lyndey's note *Marouli is Greek for lettuce. In Greece they remove the ribs from the lettuce but I don't like the waste so I use the whole leaves. Although I usually dress a salad immediately prior to serving, in Greece it is customary to dress them earlier; however, I've spoken to a couple of restaurants about this and they've said they dress it at the time of serving nowadays but that the squeezing of the lettuce leaves is the important factor.*

Cauliflower salad *Kounóupídi saláta*

SERVES 4 Preparation and cooking time 20 minutes

Trim 1 small cauliflower of its outer leaves and coarse stem. Break it into florets, and then cook them in a large saucepan of boiling salted water until just tender. Drain and place in a serving bowl. Whisk together ½ cup extra-virgin olive oil with the juice of 2 large lemons, season well with salt and freshly ground black pepper. Pour over the cauliflower to serve.

Lyndey's note *This mix of cauliflower, extra-virgin olive oil and lemon juice is very simple, yet very appealing; for the best flavour serve it while the cauliflower is still warm.*

From left: Marouli salad, Cauliflower salad, Village salad.

Fennel, artichoke and broad bean salad

Marátho, anginares kai koukia saláta

In Greece, there are many salads without a lettuce leaf in sight. The addition of different herbs makes them sing but here I have taken a liberty by adding fennel to the salad, which is not strictly traditional.

Remove the base and cut the stalk from each fennel bulb. Halve the bulbs and remove the cores. Using a sharp knife, vegetable peeler or mandolin, shave the fennel into thin slices. Place the fennel on a serving platter, add the artichoke hearts and peeled broad beans.

Drizzle with the oil, sprinkle with dill, and add freshly ground black pepper and lemon juice to taste. Top with the shaved cheese.

Lyndey's note *I don't know that peeling broad beans is very 'Greek' as typically in Greek cuisine little is wasted. However, I prefer to double peel as the bean inside is sweet and delicate, a perfect match to the shaved fennel and artichoke. To remove the skin from the inner bean, cook fresh broad beans in boiling water until just tender (don't salt the water), drain, allow to cool and slip the skin away.*

SERVES 4
Preparation and cooking time
15 minutes

4 baby fennel bulbs
8 bottled artichoke hearts, cut into halves
500 g fresh broad beans, shelled and peeled, or 250 g frozen broad beans, cooked and peeled (see Lyndey's note)
2 tablespoons extra-virgin olive oil
¼ cup dill
lemon juice to taste
80 g piece kasseri, kefalotyri cheese or pecorino, shaved

METHANA SPRINGS

Methana proved to be well named — presumably the derivation of the modern word methane with its rotten egg connotations! Here in the east Peloponnese is a series of hot sulphurous springs dating back over twenty centuries and formed by volcanic action. The springs come up through the amazingly blue sea water. Blair and I were advised to stay in the water for at least 20 minutes and not to shower for the same time to gain the full benefits the natural minerals in the waters offer. Not a popular choice with the crew!

Flying squid in garlic and olive oil

Thrápsala may skórdo kai ládi

I cooked this meal at Vivari Beach at Drepano after buying some flying squid in Nafplio market. They are seasonal and quite small; calamari such as Hawkesbury is similar, or else use small loligo squid. Otherwise use any calamari available — large ones would need to be cut up.

To clean each squid, gently pull on the tentacles to remove them. Reserve. Remove the clear quill from the body and any dark membrane and discard. The side flaps can be left on if the squid are small, or removed if large. Leave the hoods whole, rinse well and pat dry with paper towels.

Heat half the oil in a large frying pan over high heat. When hot add half the squid. After a minute or two, turn and add half the garlic. When the squid is just cooked and tender remove from heat. Repeat with remaining squid, tentacles (and flaps, if they have been removed).

Squeeze over the lemon juice and scatter with parsley. Serve immediately with crusty bread.

Lyndey's note *Small squid do not need their skin removed but to remove it from larger squid, salt the fingers to help rub it off.*

SERVES 6 as an entrée
Preparation and cooking time 25 minutes

1 kg flying squid or other small squid or calamari
¼ cup olive oil
3 garlic cloves, chopped
juice of 1 lemon
¼ cup chopped flat-leaf parsley
bread to serve

Greek yoghurt and honey
Yahórti may meli

Greek yoghurt is like no other — it is so thick and luscious. The technique used here of draining it ensures the end result is extra thick and rich. Use a good brand of Greek yoghurt for the best results.

Place two 60 cm squares of clean muslin or thin, clean cotton on top of each other in a small strainer, and place the yoghurt in the centre. Bring the corners of the muslin together. Suspend the yoghurt in the strainer over a bowl and leave to drain in the refrigerator for 24 hours.

To serve the yoghurt, use two dessertspoons to scoop out spoonfuls of yoghurt onto a serving plate. Drizzle with honey and sprinkle with the walnuts.

Lyndey's note *For a savoury version of this recipe, add 1 teaspoon salt to the yoghurt and stand for 24 hours. To serve, take 1 tablespoon of drained yoghurt and gently roll it into a ball, repeat with remaining yoghurt. Roll the balls in a mixture of fresh thyme leaves and toasted sesame seeds. Drizzle the yoghurt balls with extra-virgin olive oil and serve with pita bread as part of a meze.*

SERVES 4–6
Preparation and cooking time
5 minutes + 24 hours standing

1 kg thick Greek-style natural yoghurt
Greek honey
1 cup walnut pieces, toasted and roughly chopped

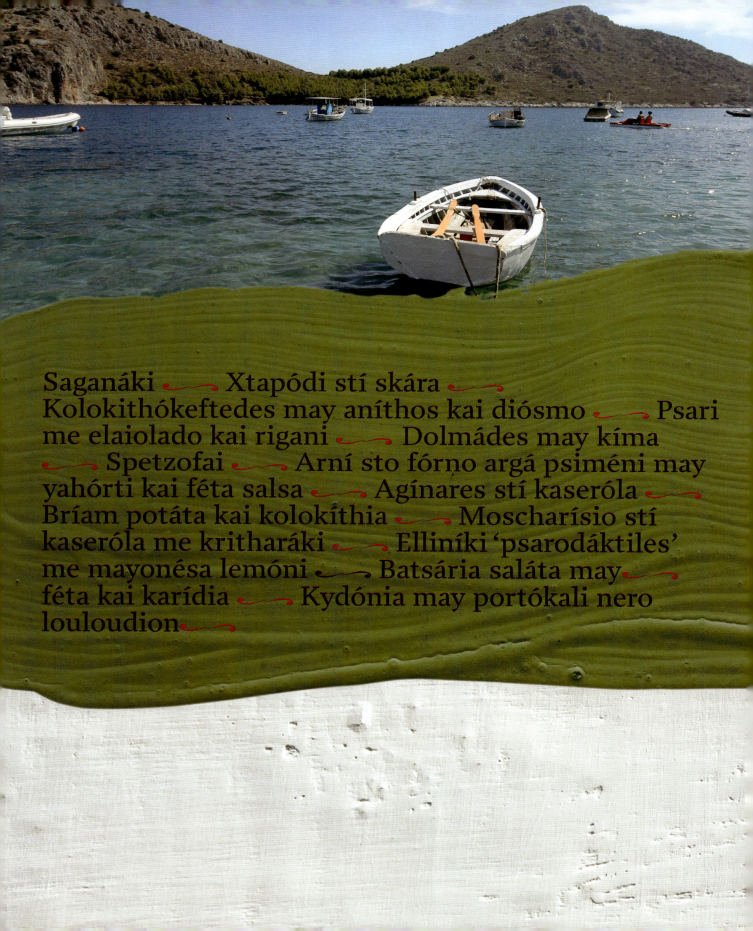

Saganáki ~ Xtapódi stí skára ~ Kolokithókeftedes may aníthos kai diósmo ~ Psari me elaiolado kai rigani ~ Dolmádes may kíma ~ Spetzofai ~ Arní sto fórno argá psiméni may yahórti kai féta salsa ~ Agínares stí kaseróla ~ Bríam potáta kai kolokíthia ~ Moscharísio stí kaseróla me kritharáki ~ Elliníki 'psarodáktiles' me mayonésa lemóni ~ Batsária saláta may féta kai karídia ~ Kydónia may portókali nero louloudion ~

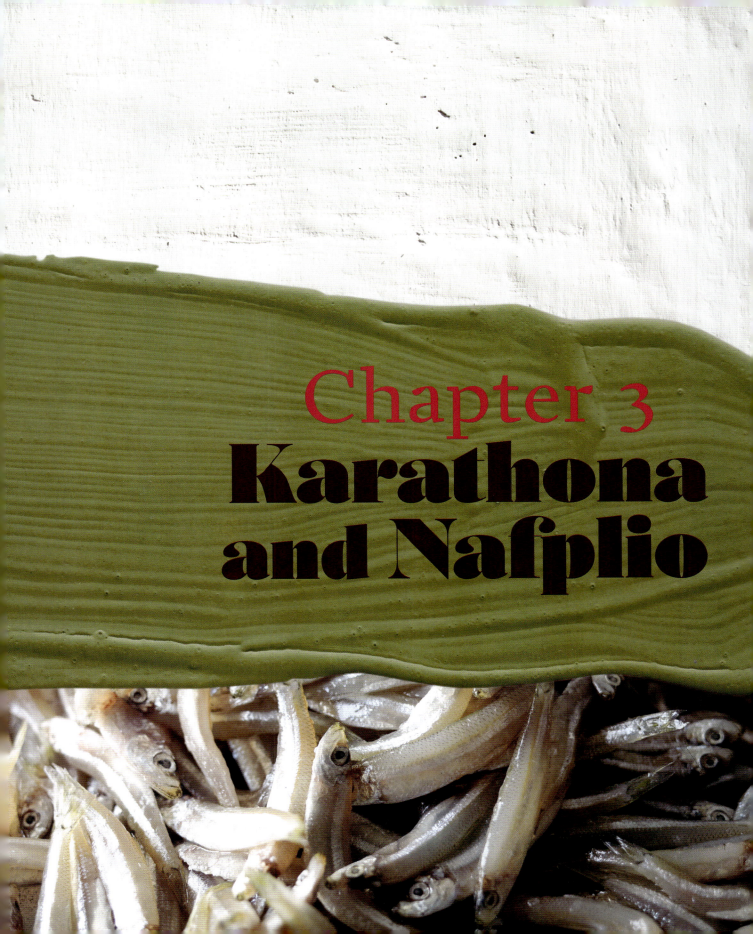

Chapter 3
Karathona and Nafplio

Nafplio is a picturesque

town of cobbled streets, alleyways and squares to sit in for a quiet coffee or a little ouzo. Visiting the nearby Karonis distillery gave us a chance to learn more about ouzo from the multi-generational family who ran it. With an ouzo or two inside him Blair was ready to set himself the challenge of running up the 999 steps of the famous Palamidi Fortress, which could be seen above the town. He did it in record time with Ben, the cameraman panting behind. I took the bus. From there the view up and down the coastline was stunning.

The next day we went to Karathona beach for lunch. By the time we got there Blair was ravenous and ended up ordering one of nearly everything on the menu. Soon Blair had his first experience of wakeboarding in Tolon. Maybe there was something lost in translation from his instructor as it wasn't his greatest triumph but he good naturedly kept trying until he got up. Again I took the quieter option and learned how to make a proper cup of Greek coffee. We were both fascinated by the museum of worry beads. Then we were supposed to cook at a waterside tavern but the best laid plans …. don't always work out. We walked around the town to find somewhere to cook and finally got lucky when we met Harris who agreed to take us to his taverna nestled in an alleyway. This was to be one of the highlights of our trip, meeting his mother Fani, a fantastic authentic cook and sister Chryssa. What luck!

Greek dips

Dips are one of the hallmarks of Greek cuisine, loved by all ages. They are served as a meze or at the beginning of a meal. While Tzatziki is the quintessential Greek dip and Blair's all-time favourite, there are many others to enjoy.

Yoghurt garlic dip *Tzatziki*

SERVES 4 as part of a meze **Preparation time** 10 minutes + overnight draining and infusing

Put 1 peeled, deseeded and finely diced telegraph or 2 medium cucumbers in a colander and sprinkle with 1 teaspoon salt. Place the colander over a large bowl. Place a plate on top of the cucumber, and then place a heavy weight on the plate. Drain overnight in the refrigerator.

Meanwhile, lay two 60 cm clean muslin squares on top of each other in a small strainer, and scoop 500 g Greek-style natural yoghurt into the centre. Bring the corners of the muslin together. Suspend the yoghurt in the strainer over a bowl and drain overnight in the refrigerator.

At the same time, put 2–3 finely chopped garlic cloves and ⅓ cup extra-virgin olive oil in a glass jar and stand to steep overnight; do not steep garlic for any longer than this.

The next day, combine the yoghurt, cucumber, garlic and garlic-infused oil and mix well. Season to taste with salt and freshly ground black pepper and add lemon juice, if you like.

Drizzle extra-virgin olive oil over the top and serve as a dip with pita bread or as a sauce for souvlaki or dolmades and cooked meats.

Split pea dip *Fáva*

SERVES 4 as part of a meze **Preparation and cooking time** 1 hour 5 minutes

---

Place 2 cups yellow split peas, 1.25 litres water and 2 finely chopped garlic cloves in a large saucepan. Bring to the boil, reduce the heat, partially cover and simmer for 1 hour, stirring from time to time. When the peas are very soft, stir to make a purée and remove from the heat. Season the purée to taste with sea salt flakes.

Serve warm or at room temperature with a drizzle of extra-virgin olive oil, wedges of red onion and some olives. If the fava thickens too much on cooling, stir in some hot water.

Feta dip *Tiri káftere*

SERVES 4 as part of a meze **Preparation time** 10 minutes

Using a food processor, chop 1 small handful mint leaves and 1 clove garlic. Crumble 200 g feta into the processor bowl, add 2 teaspoons dried chilli flakes and 250 g Greek-style natural yoghurt. Using the pulse button, process in short bursts until just combined. Season to taste with salt and freshly ground black pepper.

From left: Yoghurt garlic dip, Feta dip, Split pea dip.

Saganaki

Saganáki

Saganaki is the name of the traditional heavy Greek frying pan used to cook this firm, salty cow's cheese of the same name. A cast-iron pan or similar heavy frying pan works well too. We had this for the first time at Karathona beach and it was to prove a favourite.

Trim the cheese evenly to create a slice about 1—1.5 cm thick. Dip the cheese into a little water then dust generously with the flour.

Heat the oil in a very small heavy frying pan over medium—low heat — no hotter or the outside of the cheese will brown before the inside softens.

Carefully add the floured cheese to the oil and fry on one side for 3 minutes before turning and frying for a further 2 minutes, or until golden. Drain well on paper towels.

Serve immediately with the lemon cheeks.

Lyndey's note *Kefalotyri cheese, kefalograviera, or even haloumi could be substituted for saganaki. Each is available from speciality Greek delicatessens, and haloumi is also available in many supermarkets.*

SERVES 4 as part of a meze
Preparation and cooking time
10 minutes

100 g saganaki cheese (see Lyndey's note)
plain flour, for dusting
⅓ cup extra-virgin olive oil
lemon cheeks to serve

BOURTZI

The little Bourtzi fortress is in Nafplio harbour, close to the town. It was built by the Venetians to protect the area from pirates and invaders. Later on it was used to house the executioner of the convicts imprisoned in the Palamidi. More recently it was a hotel during the 1930s to the 1970s. Now it is a beautiful tourist attraction.

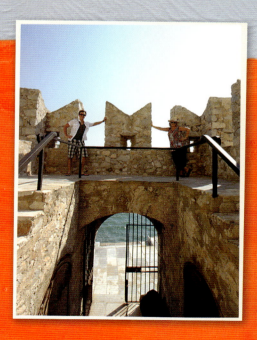

Fish with olive oil and rigani

Psari me elaiolado kai rigani

Rigani is not only used with meat. In Greece it is used with everything and has the ability to liven up the flavour of even the simplest dishes, such as this one.

Preheat the oven to 180°C (160°C fan-forced). Combine the rigani, salt, oil, lemon juice and some freshly ground black pepper in a small jug and whisk to combine.

Peel the potatoes, leaving a little of the skin on. Cut the potatoes into even-sized cubes. Arrange in a small, shallow baking dish. Scatter the garlic among the potato, if using. Add the water — it should just cover the potatoes.

Drizzle the potatoes with one-third of the oil and rigani mixture. Bake, uncovered, for 20 minutes, or until the potatoes are just tender.

Place the fish cutlets on top of the potatoes, then pour the remaining oil and rigani mixture over the fish. Add a little more water if the potatoes seem too dry. Return to the oven and bake for 10 minutes, or until the fish is just cooked through.

Lyndey's note *Any firm-fleshed fish cutlets or even-sized fish fillets can be used. If using fillets, tuck any thin ends of fish underneath the fillet to make a piece of equal thickness.*

SERVES 4
Preparation and cooking time 40 minutes

1 tablespoon rigani
2 teaspoons sea salt flakes
⅔ cup extra-virgin olive oil
juice of 2 large lemons
4 large desiree or waxy potatoes
about 300 ml water
3 garlic cloves, finely sliced (optional)
4 blue-eye cutlets (about 800 g) (see Lyndey's note)

Zucchini, dill and mint fritters

Kolokithókeftedes may aníthos kai diósmo

Vegetable fritters are very popular and may be battered and deep-fried. However, I find that shallow-frying them is more subtle and allows the full flavour of the zucchini and herbs to come out.

Coarsely grate the zucchini, sprinkle with the salt, place in a colander and stand for 30 minutes. Drain the zucchini, place in a clean tea towel or on paper towels and squeeze to remove any excess liquid.

Combine the zucchini, onion, dill, mint, oregano, flour, cheese and egg and mix well.

Heat the oil in a large, frying pan over a medium heat. Form heaped tablespoons of the zucchini mixture into small patties and fry in batches for 3–4 minutes on each side, or until golden and cooked through. Drain the fritters on paper towels. Serve immediately, with lemon wedges on the side.

Lyndey's note *Kefalotyri cheese is a hard sheep's cheese, with a sharp aroma and rich salty taste, much like the Italian-style pecorino cheese. It's a versatile cheese, good for grating, baking or just nibbling.*

MAKES about 15
Preparation and cooking time
25 minutes + 30 minutes standing

500 g (about 4) zucchini (courgettes)
3 teaspoons salt
1 small red onion, very finely chopped
½ bunch dill, finely chopped
½ bunch mint leaves, finely chopped
1 tablespoon oregano leaves, chopped
½ cup plain flour
½ cup grated kefalotyri or pecorino cheese (see Lyndey's note)
2 eggs, lightly beaten
about 1 cup Greek extra-virgin olive oil for shallow-frying
lemon wedges to serve

Meze and ouzo

In Greece, ouzo and meze are inextricably linked. No-one drinks in Greece without something to eat and, if you order ouzo, it will always come with a mezedes (small appetiser). Ouzo is an anise-flavoured spirit, distilled with anise and other flavourings and best drunk fresh or no longer than 6 to 12 months after distillation. It is either poured as a measure into a small highball glass or served in a 200 ml bottle called a karafaki (carafe), which is placed on the table with a jug of water and an ice bucket. As ice and water are added to the ouzo, it turns cloudy. Glasses are clinked and the collective toast, 'Yiamas!' (Health!) is shouted as everyone takes a drink. It creates a great atmosphere, which is known as 'kefi' in Greece.

As ouzo is considered a social drink, it is enjoyed in the company of others, and the accompanying food, meze, reflects this as it is designed to share. Meze comprises little dishes or tidbits known as mezedes, which are eaten when accompanied by ouzo or its cousins, tsipouro, raki, tsikoudia, wine or retsina. Meze can be enjoyed anytime from about 11 a.m. Before that you'd be drinking coffee.

The dishes that make up meze are generally high in fat or oil and are salty, such as feta, olives, fried fish and marinated fish. As Yiannis at the Karonis distillery explained to us, 'It is like a game of balance inside your taste.'

A typical plate might include any of the following: olives, either a local cheese or feta, some keftedes (little meatballs) some slices of tomatoes if in season, a few fried fish such as anchovies, some sliced bread cut and dipped in olive oil, tzatziki on bread, local sausage (loukaniko), local cured pork (pasto), deep-fried calamari, grilled octopus or some sort of fried vegetable balls. In the tavernas where meals are being cooked for the day you may be lucky to get some belly pork (pancetta) cooked in the oven or a few giant beans in tomato sauce.

Though there are some general similarities in the type of food offered as meze around Greece, there are regional differences. For instance, if you are in a simple village 'kafeneion' (coffeehouse), meze might just be the odd slice of tomato, cheese and a couple of olives, but if you are on the seafront it could be a pile of prawns fried in olive oil, fresh mussels and grilled octopus. Meze can be specific dishes or, if you are in a taverna, little servings of a bit of everything that's being

There's an art to meze — it is savoured, and defintely not rushed.

cooked for that day. The dishes are served in small quantities that tickle your tastebuds and complement the drink of choice.

The domain of meze used to belong to men who would gather at an ouzerie (traditional Greek tavern that serves ouzo), but now you'll see mixed groups of 'parea' or company on Sundays after church, on days of celebration or name days, out enjoying meze. Naturally, tourists to Greece love it as well.

There's an art to meze — it is savoured, and definitely not rushed. When the food arrives on the table it is surveyed and not touched. Eventually, one person will take an olive or a piece of feta and maybe others will follow suit or wait for a while. It's not cool to hurry. Usually if another round of drinks are ordered, so is more food. You can order a larger meze known as a 'pikilia' if there's a bigger crowd or you would like more variety.

During fasting times in Greece you would get a 'nistisimo' or fasting meze with no meat and no fish although shellfish is allowed as it has no blood flowing through its body.

From left: Olives marinated with lemon and fennel (page 188), Baby octopus marinated in honey (page 31), Salt cod fritters with tzatziki (page 115), Lamb keftedes (page 34).

Chargrilled octopus
Htapódi stí skára

We ate this dish at the taverna on Karathona beach. The menu declared that the octopus was out of season, thus frozen. However, since freezing actually tenderises the octopus, I wasn't concerned. This is a fantastic technique of pre-cooking the octopus first to make it really soft.

Preheat the oven to 180°C (160°C fan-forced). Wash the octopus tentacles under cold water, place them in a non-stick roasting tin, cover the tin with a layer of baking paper and then foil, and secure the edges around the roasting tin to seal it. Cook for 40–45 minutes, or until the octopus is tender when tested with a fork. Check it once or twice during the cooking time to ensure it doesn't dry out. If necessary, add a little water for moisture.

Place the tentacles in a large bowl, add the oil and squeeze over the lemon juice. Chop the lemon into quarters and add to the bowl. Add the garlic, rigiani and salt and season with some freshly ground black pepper. Cover and marinate for 30 minutes or overnight in the refrigerator.

Preheat a large barbecue flat plate or chargrill plate to hot. Drain the octopus and cook for a few minutes on each side. If the flat plate or chargrill is small, cook the octopus in two batches, reheating the plate to hot between batches.

Meanwhile, to make the slaw, combine the cabbage and carrot and dress with the wine vinegar and oil to taste.

Slice the octopus tentacles to serve. Serve with lemon wedges and the cabbage slaw.

SERVES 4–6
Preparation and cooking time
50 minutes + 30 minutes marinating

1 kg large octopus tentacles
½ cup extra-virgin olive oil
1 large lemon, cut into halves
2 garlic cloves, smashed
2 tablespoons lightly crushed rigani
2 teaspoons sea salt flakes
lemon wedges to serve

Cabbage slaw
¼ savoy cabbage, shredded
1 carrot, peeled and shredded
red or white wine vinegar to taste
extra-virgin olive oil to taste

Meat-stuffed dolmades

Dolmádes may kíma

These are the best dolmades ever! Fani, the chef at Taverna O'Pseiras in Nafplio, makes these with two types of rice — white, which absorbs more liquid and yellow, which holds its shape and prevents the stuffing becoming mushy. However, medium- or short-grain rice works well.

Blanch the vine leaves in boiling water for a couple of minutes, then refresh in batches of cold water to cool. Drain and pat dry.

To make the filling, combine the mince, onion, dill, mint, rice, salt, oil and enough water to bind the mixture.

Working one at a time, place the vine leaves on a flat surface with the ribs facing upwards and the stalk end facing towards you. Place a teaspoon of stuffing (varying slightly with the size of the leaf) towards the stalk end of the leaf. Firmly roll the stalk end over, then tuck in the sides and roll up completely. Place, seam side down, in a large casserole dish or pressure cooker. Repeat with the rest of the leaves and filling. Place the dolmades close together, in layers, so they don't unravel.

Preheat the oven to 180°C (160°C fan-forced). Season the dolmades with salt and freshly ground black pepper and pour over the tomato sauce or purée, add the water (or more if the dolmades seem dry) and oil. Top with the diced butter. Place two ovenproof dinner plates on top of the dolmades to weigh them down.

Cover and cook for about 40 minutes, or until the meat is cooked or, if cooking in a pressure cooker, remove the plates and cook for about 15 minutes.

Remove the dinner plates, add the lemon juice and serve the dolmades with some cooking liquid poured over as a sauce. Mop up with crusty bread.

Lyndey's notes To make fresh tomato sauce whizz 6 fresh tomatoes in the food processor.

In winter at the Taverna O'Pseiras, this is served with avgolemono rather than tomato sauce, made by beating together 3 eggs, 100 ml lemon juice and slowly adding in a cup of sauce removed from the cooking pot. This is then poured back over the dolmades in the pot.

MAKES 60
Preparation and cooking time
35 minutes (with a pressure cooker) or 1 hour (in the oven)

60 (about 240 g) vine leaves, fresh, frozen or vacuum-packed in brine
2 cups fresh tomato sauce or tomato purée (see Lyndey's notes)
about ½ cup water
¼ cup extra-virgin olive oil
40 g cold butter, diced
juice of 1 lemon
crusty bread to serve

Beef and rice filling
1 kg minced beef
1 large red onion, grated
½ bunch dill, finely chopped
1 handful dried spearmint, leaves rubbed between the palms or 2 tablespoons dried mint
1 cup medium- or short-grain rice (or a mix of yellow and white)
1 teaspoon salt or more to taste
100 ml extra-virgin olive oil

Spetzofai

Spetzofai

This is a traditional dish, originally from Volos in Greece and it was the second recipe I cooked at Taverna O'Pseiras, this time with Harris. It is simple yet so delicious. Any good-quality chunky sausages can be used.

Heat the oil in a large frying pan. Add the capsicums and onions and cook for 5–8 minutes, or until just softened. Remove with a slotted spoon, and place in a large saucepan, leaving the oil in the frying pan.

Add the sausages to the frying pan and cook, turning occasionally, for 3–4 minutes, or until well browned.

Transfer the sausages to the large saucepan with the capsicums and onions. Place the saucepan over a medium heat, add the processed tomatoes or tomato purée, chillies, water, salt and sugar and season with some freshly ground black pepper. Bring the mixture to simmering point, partially cover and cook for 10 minutes.

SERVES 4
Preparation and cooking time
30 minutes

- ⅓ cup extra-virgin olive oil
- 2 large red capsicums (peppers), sliced
- 2 large yellow capsicums (peppers), sliced
- 2 large green capsicums (peppers), sliced
- 3 red onions, chopped
- 6 Greek-style village sausages, sliced
- 8 large ripe tomatoes, whizzed in a food processor, or 3 cups bottled tomato purée
- 2 small dried red chillies, crumbled
- 1 cup water
- 1 teaspoon sea salt flakes
- 1 teaspoon sugar

Slow-roasted lamb ribs with yoghurt and feta sauce

Arní sto fórno argá psiméni may yahórti kai feta salsa

Lamb is glorious in Greece. We had stunning long-cut cutlets cooked over the open charcoal fire at Taverna O'Pseiras. I used that as the inspiration for this dish though using a more inexpensive cut. Cooking like this removes much of the fat.

Trim the lamb riblets of excess fat, then cut into individual ribs. Combine the oil, rigani, mint, lemon zest and some freshly ground black pepper. Rub the herb mixture over the lamb ribs and stand at room temperature for 30 minutes, or refrigerate overnight.

Preheat the oven to 160°C (140°C fan-forced). Place the lamb riblets on a rack in a roasting tin. Add a little water to the roasting tin. Season the ribs with salt and roast for 1½ hours, or until golden brown and the meat is meltingly tender.

While the lamb riblets are cooking, make the sauce. Place the yoghurt, feta, garlic, chilli flakes, mint and dill in a food processor or blender. Using the pulse button, process in short bursts until just combined. Season to taste with salt and freshly ground black pepper.

Serve the riblets with the yoghurt and feta sauce for dipping or drizzling over the meat.

Lyndey's note *Lamb riblets are cut from a square-cut shoulder of lamb. You may need to order them from your butcher. They have a good amount of juicy meat and are perfect for slow roasting. You can also use lamb ribs from the breast and flap, though they don't have has much meat. Alternatively, you could season lamb cutlets with the herb mix and chargrill until just tender and serve drizzled with the sauce.*

SERVES 6
Preparation and cooking time
1¾ hours + 30 minutes standing time

4 lamb riblet sets (with about 6 ribs in each set) (see Lyndey's note)
2 tablespoons extra-virgin olive oil
3 tablespoons rigani, lightly crushed
2 tablespoons dried mint
grated zest of 2 lemons

Yoghurt and feta sauce
250 g Greek-style natural yoghurt
200 g feta, crumbled
1 garlic clove, peeled
1 teaspoon dried red chilli flakes
1 teaspoon dried mint
½ cup dill

Braised artichokes

Aginares sti kaseróla

Artichokes were in season and plentiful when we were in Greece, so of course I had to include them in this book.

SERVES 4
Preparation and cooking time
1¼ hours

Fill a large bowl with cold water and squeeze lemon juice into the water. Work with one artichoke at a time and then place it in the water so it doesn't discolour. Prepare each artichoke by breaking off the tough outer leaves. Use a small sharp knife to peel the stem then trim to 3 cm long. Cut 2 cm from the top of the artichoke. Cut the artichoke in half lengthwise and use a teaspoon to scoop out the furry choke from the centre. Place the artichoke halves in the water bowl. Repeat with the remaining artichokes.

Preheat the oven to 180°C (160°C fan-forced). Heat the oil in a large flameproof casserole dish (one with a lid) over a medium heat. Add the onion and cook, stirring, for 1 minute until it softens but does not brown. Add the garlic and capsicum and stir for a further 1 minute.

Drain the artichoke halves and place in the casserole dish along with the potatoes, thyme and bay leaves. Add enough water or stock to cover the ingredients by about 3 cm. Cover with the lid and bake for 45 minutes, or until the artichokes are tender. Remove the lid in the last 10 minutes to evaporate a little of the braising liquid if needed. Serve hot or warm.

juice of 1 lemon
4 large fresh globe artichokes
¼ cup extra-virgin olive oil
1 large onion, chopped
3 garlic cloves, chopped
1 large red capsicum, chopped into large pieces
600 g (about 3 medium) waxy potatoes, peeled and chopped
4–6 thyme sprigs
2 bay leaves
2 teaspoons sea salt flakes
about 3 cups water or vegetable stock

Briam of potato and zucchini

Bríam potáta kai kolokíthia

Vegetables are eaten in many different ways in Greece and can be part of a meal served in the middle of the table or as a main course.

Preheat the oven to 200°C (180°C fan-forced). Combine the garlic, rosemary, dill and oil. Brush a large, shallow (about 5 cm deep), baking dish with a little of the oil.

Layer the potatoes, zucchini, tomatoes and onion in the dish, making sure each layer is evenly spread. Drizzle over a little of the oil mix and season with the salt and some freshly ground black pepper between each layer. Tuck the bay leaves into the final layer. Drizzle with remaining oil.

Bake, uncovered, for 30 minutes and reduce the heat to 180°C (160°C fan-forced) if the vegetables are browning too quickly. Drizzle the water over the vegetables and bake for a further 30 minutes, or until the vegetables are cooked and the top and edges are crisp and golden.

SERVES 4
Preparation and cooking time
1¼ hours

- 4 large garlic cloves, crushed
- 1 tablespoon rosemary leaves
- 1 tablespoon dried dill or rigani
- ¾ cup extra-virgin olive oil
- 600 g (about 3 medium) waxy potatoes, peeled
- 4 zucchini (courgettes), finely sliced lengthwise
- 2 tomatoes, finely sliced
- 1 large red onion, finely sliced
- 1 teaspoon sea salt flakes
- 3 bay leaves
- 1 cup water

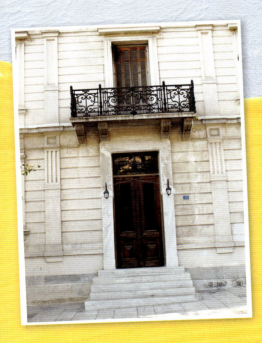

Braised veal with orzo

Moscharísio stí kaseróla me kritharáki

Pasta has its place in Greek cuisine and this comforting, yet surprisingly refined dish uses small orzo, which is much the size of rice.

Preheat the oven to 180°C (160°C fan-forced). Drizzle half of the oil over the veal cubes, mix well and season with salt and freshly ground black pepper.

Heat a large flameproof casserole dish (one with a lid) over a medium–high heat. Brown the veal in two or three batches, reheating the dish between batches.

Heat the remaining oil in the dish, add the onion and cook, stirring, for 1 minute to soften but not brown the onion. Add the garlic and stir for a further 30 seconds. Pour in the wine and let it come to the boil. Return all of the veal to the dish, then add the rigani, marjoram and 2 cups of the stock and stir to mix. Cover the dish with the lid and cook for 1 hour, stirring it once or twice.

Add the remaining stock, the tomatoes and parsley. Cook, covered, for 15 minutes before adding the orzo. Cover again, return to the oven and cook for a further 10–12 minutes, or until the orzo is just cooked. Remove the lid and sprinkle the braised veal with crumbled feta and a few parsley leaves. Serve immediately.

SERVES 4
Preparation and cooking time 1¾ hours

⅓ cup extra-virgin olive oil
1 kg veal shoulder, boned, cut into 3 cm cubes
1 large onion, chopped
3 garlic cloves, chopped
⅔ cup white wine
1 tablespoon rigani
1 tablespoon marjoram or oregano leaves
3 cups beef stock
400 g can diced tomatoes
⅓ cup flat-leaf parsley
1 cup orzo pasta
100 g feta or kefalotyri, crumbled
flat-leaf parsley to serve

PRICKLY PEAR

The prickly pear abounds in Greece and is known as fragosika, which translates as Frankish figs. This is a derogatory term with sexual connotations, reference to the fact that the prickly pear was thought to have been introduced by the invading Franks in the Middle Ages. There are many theories on how to prepare and eat them, given their thorny exterior and sharp hairs, which can get into the eyes, nose, lips and hands. One method is to collect them on a windless day, wearing thick gloves and roll them immediately in a bucket of sand to remove the hairy spines. They can then be peeled, put in the refrigerator and eaten ice cold, perfect for the hot Greek summer.

Greek 'fish fingers' with lemon mayonnaise

Ellinikí 'psarodáktiles' me mayonésa lemóni

This is a modern idea, which is a play on the idea of packaged fish fingers but with Greek flavours.

SERVES 4
Preparation and cooking time
35 minutes + 15 minutes setting

To prepare each sardine, pinch the head between your thumb and forefinger and pull it off. Rinse and pat dry with paper towels.

You can leave the sardines whole or butterfly them. To butterfuly the sardines, work one at a time. Slice down the full length of the belly to just before the tail. Place the sardine, belly side down, on a board and roll a rolling pin over it to flatten. Turn the sardine over and pull the backbone away towards the tail and discard. Repeat with the remaining sardines.

Combine the breadcrumbs, dill, oregano and salt and place on a plate. Place the flour on a separate plate. Put the egg in a small, shallow bowl with a little water; mix well.

Dust each fish in the flour, then dip in the egg, then into the breadcrumbs, making sure they are well coated with crumbs. Place on a tray for 15 minutes to set the crumbs.

To make the mayonnaise, process the egg yolks, lemon zest, juice and salt in a processer. Continue to process, adding the oil very slowly. As you add the oil the mixture will come together to form a mayonnaise.

Pour oil into a medium heavy-based saucepan to a depth of about 7 cm and place over a medium—high heat. Test the heat of the oil with a wooden implement to see if bubbles appear.

Cook the sardines in one or two batches for about 4 minutes, or until golden, then drain on paper towels. Serve immediately with the lemon mayonnaise.

24 small fresh sardines or 12 larger sardines, cleaned
2 cups fresh breadcrumbs
½ cup dill
⅓ cup oregano leaves
1 teaspoon sea salt flakes
½ cup plain flour
1 egg
extra-virgin olive oil for deep-frying

Lemon mayonnaise
2 egg yolks
grated zest of 1 lemon
1 tablespoon lemon juice
1 teaspoon sea salt flakes
½ cup extra-virgin olive oil

Salad of beetroot, feta and walnuts

Batsária saláta may feta kai karídia

On a previous visit to Greece I really enjoyed a salad of raw beetroot on Crete. The beetroot was thickly sliced and sprinkled with raw garlic. I wanted to make a more refined yet very delicious version. Perfect with barbecued lamb or seafood, Greek-style of course!

Peel the beetroot, slice and cut the slices into sheds. Pile the beetroot on a serving platter.

To make the dressing, whisk together the garlic, oil, vinegar, salt and some freshly ground black pepper.

Pour the dressing over the beetroot, then sprinkle with the walnuts and feta. Toss the salad just before serving to combine the colours and flavours.

Lyndey's note *Baby beetroot leaves can be tossed with the beetroot and feta, if you like.*

SERVES 4
Preparation and cooking time
15 minutes

3 medium beetroot
⅔ cup walnut pieces, toasted
100 g feta, crumbled

Salad dressing
2 garlic cloves, finely chopped
¼ cup olive oil
1 tablespoon red wine vinegar
1 teaspoon sea salt flakes

PALAMIDI

The Palamidi is a massive citadel that towers 999 steps above Nafplio with stunning views of the surrounding area. This truly magnificent series of fortifications was constructed by the Venetians during their occupation of the Peloponnese. Little wonder that there are still dishes on restaurant menus in Nafplio that have 999 in the title.

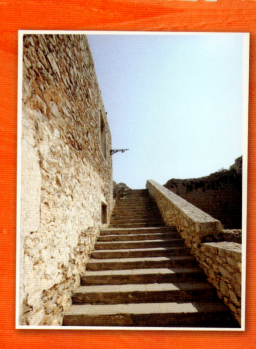

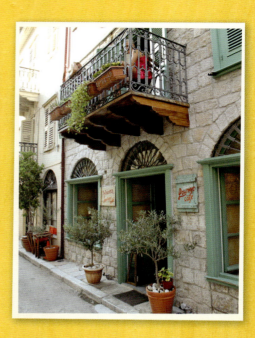

NAFPLIO

Nafplio is one of the prettiest towns on the Mediterranean. Full of quaint old buildings, restaurants and shops beside the blue sea, it also has a fascinating history. When the Greeks gained their independence this seaport became the capital for thirteen years. An important city since antiquity, it has been occupied by the Ancient Greeks, Byzantines, Franks and Venetians and finally the Ottoman Turks who were eventually starved out by the Greeks in 1821. Greece's first head of state, Ioannis Kapodistrias, was assassinated on the steps of Saint Spyridon church in Nafplio by members of another clan. Chaos ensued and order was only restored when King Otto came to power and eventually moved the capital to Athens.

Poached quinces with orange flower water

Kydónia may portókali nero louloudion

I was amazed to see quinces in the market in Greece. Although it was autumn, the weather was very hot and I think of quinces as a winter fruit. They well reward the time they take to cook. Try matching them with the Greek creamed rice (page 153).

Combine the water and sugar in a large saucepan and stir over a medium heat without boiling until the sugar dissolves, then bring to the boil for 1 minute.

Reduce the heat to low and, when the mixture is simmering, add the quinces, orange zest and lemon juice. Simmer, partially covered, for about 2 hours, or until the quinces are rosy and tender. Check from time to time, to ensure the mixture is simmering, adjusting the heat up or down as needed.

Remove the quinces from the liquid and boil the liquid to reduce to thick syrup. Add the orange flower water.

Serve the quinces warm, at room temperature or cold with a dollop of yoghurt. Drizzle with the syrup.

SERVES 4
Preparation and cooking time
2 hours 20 minutes

1.25 litres water
5 cups caster sugar
4 quinces (1.4 kg), peeled, cut into quarters and cored
2 or 3 strips orange zest
1 tablespoon lemon juice
1 teaspoon orange flower water, to taste
Greek-style natural yoghurt to serve

Melitzána saláta ~ Gígantes vrasména may tomátes ~ Kolokithókourmades may tíri tou katsíkio, tiganísmeni me ouzo ~ Papoutsákia ~ Bacaláro krokétes kai tzatzíki ~ Hortópita ~ Rozédes apo Kythéra ~ Koúmara apo Kythéra ~ Tirí tou katsíkiou, may fraóulas kai friganísmeni amígdala ~ Manóuri sti skára may síka kai méli sto fórno ~ Pásteli

Chapter 4
Monemvasia and Kythira

It was hard to leave Nafplio

but we were excited to head towards the great rock of Monemvasia. On the way we stopped for lunch at the picturesque seaside village of Plaka where we met the owner of the restaurant, an absolute find. We called him Thomas 'Please' because that's what he constantly said. He was one great guy and so proud of what his taverna showcased.

As the island of Monemvasia came into view, out came the cameras. We made our way across the causeway that links the mainland to the island and walked through a mysterious arch to find the most beautiful cobbled streets and maze of Byzantine walls unmarred by cars. It was like pulling back a curtain to a whole new world. We ended our day on a rooftop terrace, sipping chilled red wine and marvelling at the view.

Next day it was Blair's turn for an early start as once again he was in the mood for a climb, this time right to the top to see the legendary Byzantine church of Agia Sofia. He had to move quickly as we were booked on the afternoon ferry to Kythira, an island with only 3300 inhabitants but 60,000 descendants in Australia! Since Kythira is famed for having the best honey in the world, we learned all about bees and beehives and even tried honey on cheese – a fantastic combination. The honey is also an important ingredient in many local sweet specialities, which we found in a store named Stavros. That day we also had our first taste of the local firewater, fatourada.

Our last stop of the day was with a wonderful Greek–Australian couple, Kate and Lucky. Kate taught me how to make rozedes while Blair disappeared to learn all about wine making from Lucky who had created his own vineyard and wine press and was making wine under his house.

Eggplant salad
Melitzána saláta

Many cultures have their version of an eggplant dip. In Greece it is called eggplant salad and we ate it for the first time at Thomas 'Please's' restaurant, Dolphin Taverna.

SERVES 4 as part of a meze
Preparation and cooking time
50 minutes + 30 minutes standing

2 (1 kg) large eggplants (aubergines)
2 garlic cloves, peeled
2 teaspoons fennel seeds
2 teaspoons sea salt flakes
2 tablespoons extra-virgin olive oil
juice of 1 small lemon
¼ cup flat-leaf parsley
1 tablespoon chopped chives
1 teaspoon sea salt flakes, extra

To serve
extra-virgin olive oil
toasted pita bread
Greek olives

Preheat the oven to 180°C (160°C fan-forced). Prick the eggplants all over with a fork. Place the eggplants directly on an oven rack with a tray underneath the rack. Roast the eggplants for 30–40 minutes, or until they are soft, turning them once or twice. Remove from the oven and stand in a colander to drain the juices for 10 minutes.

Cover the peeled garlic with boiling water and stand for 10 minutes; this will soften the raw taste. Drain.

Toast the fennel seeds and salt flakes in a small, dry frying pan over a medium heat until fragrant. Reserve until needed.

Cut the eggplants in half, spoon the flesh into a food processor, add the garlic, oil, lemon juice, parsley, chives, extra salt and some freshly ground black pepper. Process until smooth. Taste and season as desired.

To serve, drizzle the eggplant salad with the oil, sprinkle with the toasted seeds and salt. Serve toasted pita bread and olives on the side.

Lyndey's note *Barbecuing the eggplants over white ashed coals or in a covered barbecue over indirect heat adds a wonderful smoky flavour though this is not so traditional in Greece. Cook them, turning often until they are blackened and flaky all over, and the flesh is soft.*

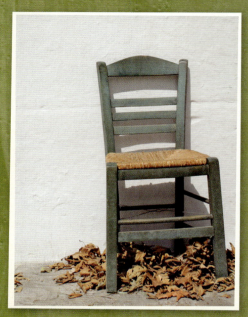

TSAKONIAN AND SPARTA

Tsakonian or Tsakonia is a dialect deriving from the ancient Doric language spoken by the Spartans in Laconia. Right up until the end of the 1920s there were some people in the eastern Peloponnese who only spoke this dialect. What's amazing is that if you understand Greek you don't necessarily understand Tsakonian as there is only about a 70 per cent crossover of language.

The whole tradition of Tsakonian has been kept alive with songs, dances and traditional costumes worn on national holidays and for local dancing displays. The dialect survived because for centuries the impassable mountains protected the locals from intruders. Now that good roads have made the area less remote, the language is under severe threat.

There are three versions of Tsakonian and only southern Tsakonian is still spoken in a handful of villages, especially those between Tyros and Leonídio. So when we ended up in Tyros for a coffee stop and happened to find the mother of the café owner spoke this language, we had to go and hear for ourselves.

Gigantes braised with tomato

Gigantes vrasména may tomátes

These were served to us by Thomas 'Please' our wonderful waiter at Plaka, near Leonidio. Greek gigantes are large round beans similar to butter beans, but larger and sweeter in flavour. Salt the beans after cooking rather than before, as this ensures the beans remain tender.

Place the beans in a large bowl and fill the bowl with cold water. Soak the beans overnight, then rinse well.

Heat the oil in a large heavy-based saucepan over a medium heat. Add the onion, carrot and celery. Cook, stirring, for 2 minutes, then add the tomato paste and cook, stirring, for a further 1 minute. Add the diced tomatoes, bay leaves, rigani, sugar, drained beans and 1.5 litres of the warm water.

Reduce the heat and simmer for up to 1½ hours, or until the beans are tender, adding the remaining warm water as needed to keep the beans just covered. Check the beans throughout the cooking time as they should be tender but still hold their shape, not get to the stage where they disintegrate.

Season well with salt and freshly ground black pepper and gently stir through the parsley leaves to serve.

If you like, pan-fry slices of the sausage and crumble over or stir through the gigantes. Serve with grilled pita bread.

Lyndey's note *Adding warm water rather than cold helps to make the beans creamy.*

SERVES 6
Preparation and cooking time
1¾ hours + overnight soaking

500 g (2½ cups) dried lima beans
¼ cup extra-virgin olive oil
1 large onion, finely chopped
1 small carrot, finely chopped
2 small celery stalks, finely chopped
½ cup tomato paste
800 g can diced tomatoes
2 bay leaves
2 tablespoons rigani
1 teaspoon sugar
about 2 litres warm water (see Lyndey's note)
1 handful flat-leaf parsley to serve
loukaniko (Greek sausage) or chorizo (optional)
grilled Greek pita bread to serve

Ouzo-battered zucchini flowers stuffed with goat's curd

Kolokithókourmades may tiri tou katsikio, tiganismeni me ouzo

Sharing meze is a wonderful, congenial way of eating. This dish is a more modern idea of battered zucchini flowers with the ouzo batter giving the deep-fried zucchini flowers a real zing.

SERVES 6 as part of a meze
Preparation and cooking time 25 minutes

To make the stuffing, combine the kefalotyri cheese, goat's curd, mint and dill and season to taste with some freshly ground black pepper.

Carefully open each zucchini flower and insert a teaspoon or two of stuffing, using your finger to push it down toward the base of the flower. Alternatively, put the stuffing in a piping bag with a large plain nozzle and pipe the stuffing into the flowers. Twist the flower a little to hold in the stuffing.

To make the batter, whisk the oil, ouzo (if using) and water into the flour and beat together well. Whisk the egg whites until frothy, then fold into the batter.

Pour plenty of oil into a medium heavy-based saucepan and place over a medium–high heat. Test the heat of the oil with a wooden implement to see if bubbles appear.

Dip the stuffed zucchini flowers one at a time into the batter, turning to coat on all sides, and then carefully place into the hot oil. Cook, turning, each zucchini flower until golden on all sides, about 3 minutes. Cook a few at a time, reheating the oil between each batch. Drain well on paper towels. Serve immediately with lemon wedges.

12 zucchini (courgette) flowers
extra-virgin olive oil for deep-frying
lemon wedges to serve

Cheese stuffing
⅔ cup grated kefalotyri or pecorino
200 g soft goat's curd
2 tablespoons finely chopped mint leaves
2 tablespoons finely chopped dill

Ouzo batter
¼ cup extra-virgin olive oil
1 tablespoon ouzo (optional)
½ cup water
½ cup plain flour
2 egg whites

Stuffed eggplants
Papoutsákia

Papoutsakia means 'little shoes' in Greek, no doubt a reference to the appearance of this dish. It is one of the many ladera (pronounced lathera) dishes, cooked with lots of good olive oil and served as a main course. Thomas 'Please' was justly proud of his version as well as the meat-free version, Iman bayildi, which translates as 'The prophet fainted', a reference to how delicious it is.

SERVES 4
Preparation and cooking time
1 hour 5 minutes

Preheat the oven to 180°C (160°C fan-forced). Line a medium baking dish with baking paper.

Halve the eggplants lengthwise and carefully scoop out the flesh, leaving a 1 cm border. Dice the flesh finely and reserve.

Heat 1 tablespoon of the oil in a large frying pan over a medium heat and cook the eggplant halves, skin side down, until wilted and slightly brown. Turn them over and cook for a further 10 minutes, or until brown. Remove from the pan and drain on paper towels. Place, cut side up, in the prepared baking dish.

Using the same frying pan, add the remaining oil. Fry the onion and garlic over low heat, stirring often. When soft, add the beef and eggplant flesh, stirring often to brown well. Add the canned tomatoes, tomato paste and, if the mixture seems a little dry, add the water. Season well with salt and freshly ground pepper. Mix well then simmer, uncovered, for 10 minutes.

Meanwhile, to make the cheese sauce, melt the butter in a small saucepan over a medium–low heat until it froths. Add the flour and stir for 2 minutes. Gradually pour in the milk, whisking constantly until the mixture comes to the boil and is thick and smooth. Add the nutmeg, egg yolk and cheese. Whisk until smooth.

Spoon the meat mixture equally into the eggplant halves, pressing in firmly. Pour over the cheese sauce and bake for 30–35 minutes, or until heated through and the tops are golden.

2 medium (600 g) eggplants (aubergines)
¼ cup extra-virgin olive oil
1 onion, finely chopped
2 garlic cloves, finely chopped
250 g minced beef
200 g canned tomatoes
2 tablespoons tomato paste
½ cup water (optional)

Cheese sauce
20 g butter
1 tablespoon plain flour
1 cup milk
pinch of ground nutmeg
1 egg yolk, beaten
1 cup grated cheese, such as kefalotyri, keflograviera, kasseri, pecorino or parmesan

MONEMVASIA

Considered the Gibraltar of Greece, Monemvasia was separated from the mainland by an earthquake in AD 375. It was occupied by the Byzantines for 700 years and today it is like stepping back into that world as every building in the old town can only be renovated in traditional style. In English history Monemvasia was known as Malmsey, after the grape that was grown there, the Malvasia grape and it is thought that this was an important port for wine trading in the Middle Ages. Several thousand New Zealand troops were evacuated from there during World War II.

Salt cod fritters with tzatziki

Bacaláro krokétes kai tzatziki

Salt cod is popular everywhere in the Mediterranean where salting is a time-honoured method for preserving fish. In Greece salt cod is even used for fish and chips, but I prefer to use it in fritters. Be sure to start your preparation for this the day before you want to eat it. (Picture on page 85.)

SERVES 4–6 as part of a meze
Preparation and cooking time
50 minutes + 24 hours soaking

Prepare the salt cod by standing it in a large bowl of water and leaving it to soak for 24 hours. Change the water two or three times at least.

Drain the cod then cut it into three or more manageable pieces. Place it in a large saucepan, add enough water to just cover, and then add the milk. Place the pan over a low heat and simmer for 20–25 minutes, or until the cod flakes easily when tested with a fork.

Meanwhile, boil the whole potatoes until tender. Cool, then peel and mash well.

Drain the cod and, when cool enough to handle, remove the skin, flaking the fish into a bowl. Take care to remove any bones.

Combine the flaked cod, mashed potato, garlic, parsley, mint, dill, green onions and eggs and season with freshly ground black pepper. Mix well.

Heat the oil in a large frying pan over a medium heat. Form heaped tablespoons of the mixture into small patties, dust the patties with flour and fry for 3–4 minutes on each side, or until golden and cooked through. Drain the fritters on paper towels. Serve immediately, with lemon wedges on the side and a dollop of tzaztiki.

1 kg dried salt cod
2 cups milk
600 g (about 3 medium) potatoes
4 garlic cloves, finely chopped
1 cup flat-leaf parsley, chopped
½ cup mint leaves, chopped
¾ cup dill, chopped
6 green onions (shallots), finely sliced, including the green sections
2 eggs, lightly beaten
1 cup extra-virgin olive oil
plain flour, for dusting
lemon wedges and tzatziki (page 74) to serve

Wild greens pie
Hortópita

Greece is legendary for its health-giving wild greens. Tuscan cabbage, chicory, watercress and rocket all contribute a slightly bitter flavour to the filling of this pie. The saltiness of the feta and sweetness of the currants offset the bitterness, and the result is wonderfully balanced. This pie is great for a picnic or to feed a crowd.

Chop the cavolo nero, chicory, watercress and rocket, place in a large colander and wash well, then drain. Heat the oil in a large, deep frying pan over a medium heat, add the leek and cook, stirring, for 1 minute to soften. Add the greens and cook, stirring occasionally, for 5 minutes. Place the cooked greens in the colander over a large bowl to drain and cool.

While the greens drain, make the pastry. Work the flour, salt, oil, egg and water together in a large bowl or food processor. Wrap the dough in plastic wrap and rest in the refrigerator for 30 minutes.

Preheat the oven to 200°C (180°C fan-forced). Take the pastry out of the refrigerator so it warms up a little, making it easier to roll. Squeeze the greens to remove any remaining liquid — they should be fairly dry. Combine the greens with the feta, mint, green onions, currants and lemon zest. Season well with salt and freshly ground black pepper.

Take two-thirds of the pastry and roll it out thinly to fit the base and side of a non-stick, shallow, 26—28 cm round tin (one with a removable base is best). Place the filling evenly over the base. Brush a little of the egg glaze around the rim of the pastry.

Roll the remaining pastry out to a thin round that is large enough to cover the top of the pie. Ease the pastry over the filling. Trim, and then seal the edge by crimping the pastry together. Make a small slash in the top of the pastry for steam to escape. Brush with the egg glaze, then sprinkle with sesame seeds and a little sea salt, if using.

Bake for 40—45 minutes, or until the pastry is golden. Stand for 10 minutes before cutting. Serve hot, warm or cold. This pie goes really well with tzatziki (page 74).

SERVES 8
Preparation and cooking time
1 hour 20 minutes + 30 minutes resting

Wild greens filling
1 bunch cavolo nero (Tuscan cabbage) or ½ bunch silverbeet (Swiss chard)
1 bunch chicory, trimmed to leaf
1 bunch watercress, trimmed to leaf
1 bunch rocket, trimmed
2 tablespoons extra-virgin olive oil
1 small leek, finely sliced
200 g feta, crumbled
1 cup mint leaves, roughly chopped
2 green onions (shallots), finely chopped
½ cup currants, soaked in warm water and drained
grated zest of 1 lemon

Olive oil pastry
3⅓ cups plain flour
1 teaspoon salt
⅓ cup extra-virgin olive oil
1 egg, lightly beaten
¾ cup cold water

Egg glaze
1 egg, whisked with a little water
1 tablespoon sesame seeds
pinch of sea salt flakes (optional)

Rozedes

Rozédes apo Kythéra

I made these with Kate on Kythira. They are traditional sweets, a specialty of the island, featuring its legendary honey. They are really more like a biscuit, crisp on the outside and chewy on the inside. For a firmer biscuit, after 20 minutes in the oven, reduce the temperature to 160°C and cook for a further 10 minutes.

MAKES 25
Preparation and cooking time
30 minutes

Preheat the oven to 180°C (160°C fan-forced) and line a large baking tray with baking paper.

Combine the almonds, sugar, honey, semolina, breadcrumbs, cloves and cinnamon in a large bowl. Add the hot water gradually, mixing until the dough is firm.

Using a dessertspoon, shape the dough into oval-shaped logs, squeezing well with your hands. Place on the prepared baking tray and bake for 20 minutes, or until firm on the outside. Remove from the oven and allow to cool for at least 20 minutes.

Pour the dessert wine into a shallow bowl and divide the icing sugar into two separate shallow bowls. Dip the biscuits briefly in the dessert wine, toss in the icing sugar, shake and then dip into the second bowl of icing sugar and toss until well coated. Set aside before serving for at least 15 minutes to allow the icing sugar to harden.

Lyndey's note *Double dipping in icing sugar gives these biscuits a traditional sugary crust. If on the first dipping, the icing sugar is absorbed by the wine, you can wait 15 minutes until you re-dip the biscuits.*

400 g unskinned almonds, ground but not as finely as almond meal
½ cup sugar
⅓ cup honey
⅓ cup fine semolina
⅓ cup dry breadcrumbs
½ teaspoon ground cloves
1 teaspoon ground cinnamon
½ cup hot water
about 1 cup clear sweet liqueur (e.g. mastica or dessert wine)
about 1¼ cups icing sugar

Kythirian koumara
Koúmara apo Kythéra

We tried these little sweets in Stavros' shop where they were made by women in the village. It's hard to believe that these tasty chocolate bites are classed as a 'fasting' food in Kythira because they contain no olive oil. Traditionally, the last week of Lent is seen as a 'fasting' week with no oil, meat, fish or dairy products.

Put the ground almonds, sugar, semolina, honey, cinnamon, ouzo and melted chocolate in a small bowl and stir the mixture until well combined.

Line a baking tray with baking paper. Wet your hands and take small pieces of the dough and roll into balls (about the size of a small walnut). Roll the balls in the chopped almonds, flatten and taper the ends a little.

Place the koumara on the tray to firm up. To keep them longer, put them in the refrigerator.

MAKES about 20
Preparation time 20 minutes

1 cup ground almonds
¼ cup caster sugar
1 tablespoon fine semolina
2 tablespoons honey
2 teaspoons ground cinnamon
2 tablespoons ouzo or brandy
180 g dark chocolate, melted
½ cup finely chopped almonds

Goat's curd with strawberries and toasted almonds

Tirí tou katsikiou, may fraóulas kai friganísmeni amígdala

Goats abound in Greece and are used for their meat and their milk. Here the very first stage of the cheese, the soft curd, makes a wonderful modern dessert.

Heat the sugar and strawberries in a large frying pan over a medium heat, shaking the pan to coat the strawberries in the sugar. Add the orange zest, juice and cinnamon and gently simmer until the sugar has dissolved, then remove from the heat and cool.

Beat the cream and icing sugar together until soft peaks form, then fold in the goat's curd.

Assemble by spooning a little of the goat's curd mixture into the bottom of four 1-cup glasses. Add a spoonful of strawberries and syrup, then more curd mixture. (Depending on the width of your glasses, you may be able to top with another layer.) Finish with the strawberries. Refrigerate for 20 minutes to firm. Sprinkle with toasted almonds to serve.

Lyndey's note *Blueberries or chopped fresh figs could replace the strawberries.*

SERVES 4
Preparation time
15 minutes + 20 minutes refrigeration

½ cup sugar
300 g strawberries, cut into quarters (see Lyndey's note)
very finely shredded zest and juice of 1 large orange
pinch of ground cinnamon
1 cup cream
1 tablespoon icing sugar
125 g goat's curd
⅓ cup flaked almonds, toasted, to serve

Chargrilled manouri served with honey-baked peaches

Manoúri sti skára may rodakina kai méli sto fórno

Manouri is a semi-soft sheep's or goat's cheese often made from the whey left over from the production of feta. It is mild, slightly sweet and utterly delicious. It is available from Greek delicatessens. If you're unable to source it, use Italian-style ricotta salata — it's a little saltier, but will still go nicely with the peaches and walnuts here.

SERVES 4
Preparation and cooking time 25 minutes

Place the manouri on paper towels on a plate and keep in the refrigerator until needed.

Preheat the oven to 180°C (160°C fan-forced). To make the syrup, heat the honey, water, lemon juice and fennel seeds in a small saucepan over a medium heat, stirring to combine, and slowly bring to the boil. Reduce the heat to low and simmer for 5 minutes.

Cut each peach in half then place in a baking dish that allows the peaches to fit snugly. Pour the syrup over the peaches and bake for 10–15 minutes, or until tender. Remove and discard the pits.

To serve, preheat a small chargrill pan to hot. Brush both sides of the manouri slices with a little of the oil. Chargrill the manouri slices on each side for 1–2 minutes. Place the manouri on the serving plates and add the warm peaches. Drizzle with syrup and sprinkle with walnuts.

Lyndey's notes *If you prefer, warm the manouri in the oven while the peaches bake. Place the manouri on a baking tray lined with baking paper and bake for 5 minutes.*

If fresh figs are in season, they are also luscious in this dish. Use 8 large fresh figs and cut them into quarters, leaving them attached at the base. Cook in the same way as the peaches.

400 g piece of manouri, cut into 4 slices
⅓ cup honey
1 cup water
juice of 1 lemon
½ teaspoon fennel seeds, lightly crushed or chopped
6 peaches (see Lyndey's notes)
olive oil for brushing
1 cup walnut pieces, toasted

KYTHIRA AND KANGAROOITSAS

'Little Australia' is how Greeks often refer to Kythira and 'Kangarooitsas' are the Greek Australians who live there and elsewhere. The island has a population of just over 3000 but there are thought to be up to 60,000 Greeks of Kythiran descent living in Australia. They flood back to the island in the summer. An Australian–Greek told me, 'When the Greeks are in Australia, all they do is talk about their beloved Kythira, but when they're here, all they do is expound about how wonderful life is in Australia! It's the Greek character.'

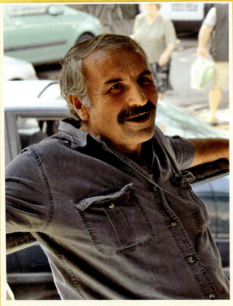

Sesame bars

Pásteli

These are one of the cornerstones of Greek confectionery and traditionally consist only of sesame seeds baked with honey. However, Greece has an abundance of almonds, too, and they make a wonderful addition. They can be cut into squares or rectangles but I think triangles are prettier.

Preheat the oven to 180°C (160°C fan-forced). Line a large slab tin (30 x 40 cm) with a sheet of baking paper, leaving the paper to extend over the sides of the tin. Place the sesame seeds and almonds over the baking paper and bake until lightly golden.

Meanwhile, place the honey in a small saucepan and bring to the boil. Reduce the heat a little and cook the honey until it turns a deeper caramel colour. Test by dropping a small spoonful into a glass of cold water; the honey should form solid threads that are flexible, not brittle.

Working quickly and carefully, add the warm toasted sesame seeds and almonds to the honey. Stir to mix, then pour into the lined slab tin. Spread the mixture out with a spatula to a uniform thickness of about 3–4 mm and press down to flatten.

Allow to cool a little then, using the baking paper, lift the pasteli from the tin and place on a large board. Use a heavy knife to score into strips, then squares and then into triangles. When cooler, cut through the markings. Store in an airtight container with baking paper between layers — they will keep for quite a long time.

Lyndey's note *To make measuring the honey easy, brush or spray the measuring cup with oil first and the honey will easily slide off.*

MAKES about 40 small squares or triangles
Preparation and cooking time 15 minutes + cooling

1½ cups sesame seeds
½ cup slivered almonds
1 cup honey (see Lyndey's note)

Gavros marinátos ❧ Angináres may koukía kai lemóni ❧ Melitzána stí kaseróla me máratho kai tomáta ❧ Kakávia ❧ Psaròsoupa Mesògio ❧ Hiríno sto fórno may patátas lemonáto ❧ Kotópolo sto fórno Pelopónissou ❧ Hiríno kai tomáta sti kasérola may skórdo kai karídia pskóla ❧ Arní sto fórno psiméni árga may saláta mavromátika kai meróudia ❧ Fasólia sti kasérola me patátas ❧ Piláfi seskoulo ❧ Fákes kai revíthia saláta ❧ Díples ❧ Rizógalos

Chapter 5
Kalogria, Stoupa and Inner Mani

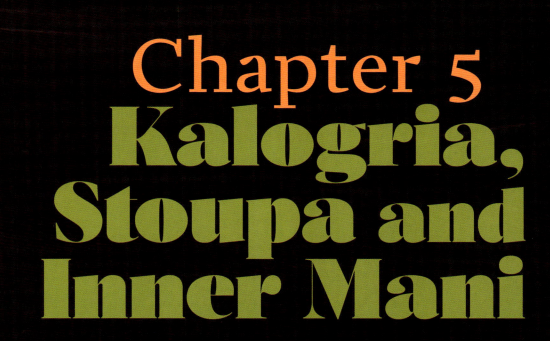

While the Mani is a region

with a reputation for fierce warriors, we found it to be a hidden gem of gorgeous scenery and beaches, made all the more special as it was home to our fabulous researcher, Pam. Through her we met her friend, Dimitris, not only a tavern owner, but a very proud fisherman. He took us out on his boat to show us an extraordinary natural phenomenon: a freshwater spring that comes down from the mountain tops and surfaces about 100 metres offshore. Ever the water baby, Blair dived straight in and was surprised both by how cold the water was and how buoyant as the spring water rose to the surface. It was just the thing to stimulate his appetite, so we were off to To Palio Bostani, Dimitris' taverna to learn the secrets of kakavia, the traditional Greek fishermen's soup that was a precursor to French bouillabaisse.

Dimitris surprised us by arranging for us to learn Greek dancing on the beach where the real Zorba the Greek had danced all those years ago. Blair thought he had learned the zeibekiko previously but this was the real deal and he delighted all with his enthusiasm and talent. We wished we could have stayed longer.

Morning found us at a local gypsy market where we could shop before eating our best breakfast ever: whole roast pig bought from a massive wooden trolley right out on the street. A man with a huge cleaver chopped so close to his hand I had to look away but it was delicious, especially the crackling.

The next day we took a boat trip through the underground caves of Diros, a beautiful spot, like a movie set and incredibly peaceful. Then I met up with Dimitris' mother and other village ladies to make diples. I was glad to be in the kitchen rather than with Blair hiking down a gorge in the heat. He revelled in the silence though he really needed some help with his map-reading skills.

Fried pumpkin balls

Kolokithókeftedes

Vegetable balls like these are popular all over the Peloponnese. However, these ones, taught to me by Dimitris and Georgia, the cook at To Palio Bostani in Kalogria, were the lightest we tried. They can be rolled small as finger food, or cooked in larger, flatter patties as a starter or part of a meze. A food processor is great for grating the pumpkin.

Combine the pumpkin, green onions, mint, parsley and flour and mix well. Season well with salt and freshly ground black pepper.

Heat the oil in a large, deep, frying pan over a medium heat. Form heaped tablespoons of pumpkin mixture into flat patties and fry for 3–4 minutes on each side, or until golden and cooked through. Serve immediately.

Lyndey's note It is important to use a firm pumpkin for this recipe; butternut pumpkin is not suitable.

MAKES 30 balls
Preparation and cooking time 20 minutes

- 1 kg firm pumpkin (e.g. Queensland blue), grated and squeezed dry (see Lyndey's note)
- 5 green onions (shallots), finely sliced
- 1 bunch mint leaves, finely chopped
- 1 bunch flat-leaf parsley, finely chopped
- 1 cup plain flour
- 1 cup extra-virgin olive oil for frying

Marinated anchovies

Gavros marinátos

These little morsels are lovely served with ice-cold beer, ouzo or tsipouro, a distilled grape liqueur. Georgia's fingers flew as she cleaned these little fish. I found it was not quite as easy as it looked!

To prepare the anchovies, pinch the head between your thumb and forefinger and pull it off and discard it with the innards (the innards should come away too), then cut off the tail and slip out the backbone, rinse (if necessary) and pat dry.

Combine the anchovies, vinegar and salt in a small, shallow, glass dish. Mix well, then cover and refrigerate for 24 hours.

Remove the anchovies from the vinegar mixture with a slotted spoon and serve topped with sliced garlic and parsley. Add a spoonful of the vinegar mixture, if you wish.

SERVES 4 as part of a meze
Preparation and cooking time
10 minutes + 24 hours marinating

250 g gavros (anchovies)
1 cup wine vinegar or to cover
⅓ cup sea salt flakes
finely sliced garlic to serve
chopped flat-leaf parsley to serve

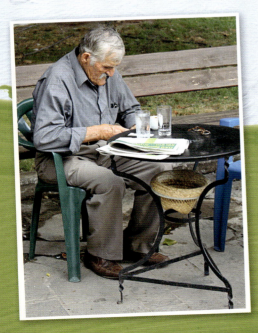

Artichokes with broad beans and lemon

Angináres may koukía kai lemóni

Vegetables are plentiful on the Greek table and are generally prepared using tomato or lemon, depending on the season. Lemon works especially well with artichokes.

Fill a large bowl with cold water and one-third of the lemon juice. Work with one artichoke at a time and then place it in the water so it doesn't discolour. Prepare each artichoke by breaking off the tough outer leaves. Use a small sharp knife to peel the stem then trim to 3 cm long. Cut 2 cm from the top of the artichoke. Cut the artichoke in half lengthwise and use a teaspoon to scoop out the furry choke from the centre. Place the artichoke halves in the water bowl. Repeat with the remaining artichokes.

Preheat the oven to 180°C (160°C fan-forced). Heat the oil in a large flameproof casserole dish (one with a lid) over a medium heat. Add the onion and cook, stirring, for 1 minute to soften but not brown. Add the garlic and leek and stir for a further 2 minutes.

Drain the artichoke halves and place in the casserole dish with the remaining lemon juice and the bay leaves. Add enough water to cover the ingredients by about 3 cm. Cover the dish with the lid and cook in the oven for 25 minutes, or until the artichokes are tender. Remove the lid for the last 5 minutes of cooking time to evaporate a little of the braising liquid, if needed. Stir through the broad beans at the end. Serve hot or warm, seasoned with salt and freshly ground black pepper and extra-virgin olive oil.

Lyndey's note *If you have a bottle of white wine open, add a splash of wine to the dish when braising.*

SERVES 6
Preparation and cooking time
1 hour 10 minutes

juice of 2 lemons
6 large fresh globe artichokes
¼ cup extra-virgin olive oil
1 onion, chopped
3 garlic cloves, chopped
1 small leek, trimmed, cut into quarters and then into 3 cm long pieces
2 bay leaves
750 g fresh broad beans, podded and peeled
about 1 cup water
extra-virgin olive oil to serve

DIROS CAVES

Nothing prepared us for the Diros caves. They simply took our breath away. Imagine gliding silently through the passageways of an underground lake, stalactites dripping above, stalagmites rising from the water. Like an underground fairyland with a constant temperature of 16–20°C. It's amazing to think that fossils more than two million years old have been discovered here and the human artefacts in the caves date back to Paleolithic and Neolithic times. The first cave was discovered around 1900. The second cave was discovered by chance in 1958 when a couple came across a foxhole. It led to the discovery of the Alepotripa cave (appropriately called foxhole) and an underground labyrinth of 6500 square metres. The full extent of the underwater labyrinth is still being explored.

Braised eggplant and fresh fennel with tomato and fennel seed

Melitzána stí kaseróla me máratho kai tomáta

Though eggplant and tomato feature in other cuisines, the addition of fennel and dill makes them feel Greek.

SERVES 4
Preparation and cooking time
50 minutes

Preheat the oven to 180°C (160°C fan-forced). Heat 30 ml of the oil in a large flameproof casserole dish (one with a lid) over a medium–high heat. Brown half the eggplants, remove from the dish then repeat with the remaining eggplant. Cook the fennel in the same dish until just starting to colour, then remove from the dish.

Add the remaining oil to the dish, reduce the heat to medium, add the onion and cook, stirring, for 1 minute to soften but not brown the onion. Add the garlic and fennel seeds and stir for a further 1 minute.

Arrange the eggplant and fennel in the dish, add the tomato purée and water. Season with the salt, sugar and a little freshly ground black pepper. Cover the dish with the lid, place in the oven and cook for 25–30 minutes, or until the eggplants and fennel are tender. Remove the lid for the last 10–15 minutes cooking time to evaporate a little of the braising liquid, if needed.

Serve warm, sprinkled with chopped dill sprigs.

100 ml extra-virgin olive oil
6 lady finger eggplants (aubergines), cut into halves lengthwise
6 baby fennel, cut into quarters
1 onion, chopped
2 garlic cloves, chopped
2–3 teaspoons fennel seeds, to taste
1 cup tomato purée
1½ cups water
1 teaspoon sea salt flakes
1 teaspoon sugar
chopped dill or fennel fronds to serve

Traditional fishermen's soup

Kakávia

Kakavia is traditional fishermen's soup, as cooked on the fishing boats. Any fish except oily ones are used — even fish half eaten by larger fish — as it all adds to the mix. Greece is blessed with wonderful olive oil, so fishermen are liberal with it in this soup — add to your taste. While red onions are traditional, white or brown give a more subtle colour to the soup.

Pour the stock into a large saucepan and add the carrots, potatoes, onions, celery, parsley and oil. Top up with water if necessary to cover the vegetables. Simmer over a medium–low heat for 20 minutes, or until the potatoes begin to soften.

Add the larger fish and cook gently for 5 minutes, then add the smaller fish and cook for a further 5 minutes. It is important that the fish are not overcooked, so they remain whole and do not disintegrate.

Carefully remove the large and small fish with a slotted spoon. Debone, discarding the bones. If you prefer, save some of the small whole fish to place on top as a garnish.

Add the fish flesh to the stock and vegetables and reheat gently. Season to taste with salt and freshly ground black pepper, then add the extra parsley. Place a piece of bread in the bottom of each individual soup bowl and ladle over the soup.

Lyndey's note To make your own fish stock, put 1 kg white fish bones and heads in a large stockpot with 3 slices lemon, 1 peeled and quartered brown onion, 1 small carrot, 1 bay leaf, a few black peppercorns and some parsley stalks, then pour in enough cold water to just cover the ingredients. Bring to the boil, reduce the heat and simmer for 20 minutes, skimming occasionally. Strain and use as needed.

SERVES 8 as part of a meal,
6 as a main
Preparation and cooking time
55 minutes

- 1 litre fish stock (see Lyndey's note)
- 2 large carrots, peeled and sliced
- 600 g (3 medium) potatoes, peeled and cut into 1–1.5 cm dice
- 2 red or white onions, finely sliced
- 2 celery stalks, sliced
- 3 flat-leaf parsley sprigs, roughly chopped
- ½ cup extra-virgin olive oil or to taste
- 2 kg mixed whole fresh fish (both large and small fish)
- torn flat-leaf parsley, extra, to taste
- 6 slices stale country-style bread or 3 bread rolls, cut into halves

ZORBA AND KALOGRIA

Who could forget the character of Zorba the Greek, brought to life by the unforgettable Anthony Quinn? Tall, gangly intellectual Nikos Kazantzakis came to run a lignite (a form of low-grade coal) mine in Stoupa during World War I and he employed as his foreman the short, energetic Alexis Zorbas. The lignite was sent down to Kalogria beach, where Zorba lived, and sent away to Kalamata on boats (as there was no road at the time). They formed a strong relationship and it is on this beach that Zorba danced, enthused by life (and perhaps a little bit by the amber nectar). Kazantzakis eventually moved to the island of Crete, where he wrote the book *Zorba the Greek* and changed the venue to Crete. However, Kalogria is where it all really happened and it was on this beach we danced too.

Mediterranean fish soup

Psaròsoupa Mesògio

This is a modern fish soup inspired by the traditional kakavia made at Dimitris' taverna, To Palio Bostani, using Greek ingredients for authentic flavour but in a fast and easy contemporary manner.

Heat the oil in a large saucepan over a medium heat, add the sliced fennel bulb and garlic and cook, stirring, for 6 minutes, or until softened, making sure not to colour. Add the tomatoes, stock, wine and lemon zest. Season with salt and bring to the boil.

Meanwhile, gently slash the skin on the snapper fillets on the diagonal — this prevents the fish from curling. Cut each fillet into four pieces.

Reduce the heat of the stock and fennel mixture and add the ouzo and marinara mix. Gently lay the prepared snapper on top. Simmer for 3 minutes, or until the fish is opaque. Season to taste with salt and freshly ground black pepper.

Ladle into soup bowls, topping each with some snapper and reserved finely chopped fennel tops.

Lyndey's note *Ouzo is traditional in Greece; however, Pernod or another aniseed-flavoured liqueur can be used.*

SERVES 4
Preparation and cooking time
30 minutes

- 1 tablespoon extra-virgin olive oil
- 1 fennel bulb, finely sliced, tips reserved and finely chopped
- 2 garlic cloves, finely sliced
- 3 tomatoes, peeled, seeded and finely diced
- 3 cups fish stock
- ¼ cup white wine
- 2 strips lemon zest
- 185 g red snapper fillets or other beautiful fish fillet, skin on
- 1½ tablespoons ouzo (see Lyndey's note)
- 350 g good-quality fresh marinara mix

Roast pork with lemon potatoes

Híríno sto fórno may patátas lemonáto

This is a do-at-home version of the most amazing whole roast pigs we saw at Messene market near Kalamata. They were set out on huge boards and the vendors cut big chunks with sharp cleavers. I was determined to work out my own way of doing it.

Talk to your butcher about this cut of pork. I found Peter's Meats, who have national distribution, very helpful. The idea is to get a half saddle (that is, the loin still with the belly attached) in a size that will fit in your oven. Measure your oven first and tell the butcher what size.

Preheat the oven to 170°C (150°C fan-forced). Lay the pork on a rack in a large, deep roasting tin.

Combine the lemon juice and oil. Brush the pork cavity with some of this mixture using the oregano as a brush. Turn the pork over so the skin is uppermost and poke the lemon skins underneath the skin. Place a meat thermometer in the thickest part of the pork. Add the salt to the lemon–oil mixture. Baste the exterior of the pork with this mixture. Roast the pork for 1 hour.

Meanwhile, to make the potatoes, place the potatoes in a baking dish and pour over the lemon juice, oil and stock.

After the first hour, increase the heat of the oven to 190°C (170°C fan-forced) and put the potatoes in the oven. After 30 minutes, stir the potatoes. If the top of the pork is uneven, you may need to rotate the roasting tin to ensure even browning.

After 2 hours total cooking time, check the pork and stir the potatoes. Increase the temperature to 200°C (180°C fan-forced) and return the pork and potatoes to the oven for a further 30 minutes or continue to cook until done. If the crackling is not looking crisp enough, increase the temperature to 240°C (220°C fan-forced) for the final 10 minutes of cooking.

Remove the pork from the oven to rest for 10 minutes. Sprinkle with rigani and season with salt and freshly ground black pepper. Use a cleaver to cut into large chunks and serve.

Lyndey's note Using a meat thermometer makes it easy to judge how well meat is cooked. The internal temperature of the pork should be 63–70°C for medium and 72–75°C for well done.

SERVES 20
Preparation and cooking time
3¾ hours + 10 minutes resting

- 1 pork loin with flap on (around 5 kg)
- ¼ cup lemon juice, about 2 lemons, skins reserved
- 30 ml extra-virgin olive oil
- 1 bunch oregano
- 1 teaspoon salt
- rigani

Lemon potatoes
- 8 (1.6 kg) potatoes, peeled and cut into quarters lengthwise
- ¼ cup lemon juice, about 2 lemons, skins reserved
- ¼ cup extra-virgin olive oil
- ½ cup chicken stock or water

Peloponnesian-style roast chicken

Kotópolo sto fórno Pelopónissou

Simple as this recipe is, it's stunning. It's basically roast chicken with lemon juice, rigani or oregano and olive oil. It's on nearly every menu in the tavernas around the Peloponnese. Team it with silverbeet pilaf (page 148) for a fabulous meal.

Preheat the oven to 200°C (180°C fan-forced.) Wash the chicken well, remove any excess fat from inside the neck cavity and remove any giblets and neck. Pat dry inside and out with paper towels.

Place the lemon quarters and garlic inside the chicken cavity. Combine the oil, lemon zest, salt, sugar and rigani in a small bowl. Rub the mixture all over the chicken. Slide two fingers between the skin and the breast and rub some of the oil mixture under the skin and over the breast.

Place the chicken in a large roasting tin and cook for 20 minutes. Pour the stock around the chicken in the roasting tin. Cook, basting once or twice with the pan juices, for a further 50 minutes, or until the chicken is cooked through. Remove from the oven, cover loosely with foil and stand for 10 minutes before serving.

SERVES 4–6
Preparation and cooking time
1 hour 20 minutes + 10 minutes resting

1.7 kg chicken
1 lemon, cut into quarters
2 garlic cloves, peeled and sliced
⅓ cup extra-virgin olive oil
2 teaspoons grated lemon zest
2 teaspoons sea salt flakes
1 teaspoon sugar
1 tablespoon rigani
⅓ cup chicken stock

Stewed pork and tomato, with garlic walnut crumb

Hiríno kai tomáta sti kasérola may skórdo kai karídia pskóla

This is my interpretation of lagoto, a richly flavoured pork stew, a speciality of the Peloponnese. Traditionally, quite a lot of garlic is used, six cloves or more (though I've halved that), and it is added at the end of the cooking time so its flavour is very intense. For a more gentle garlic flavour, I've cooked it with the pork at the beginning of the braising time. I've also chosen to toast the crumb and walnut mixture used to thicken the dish at the end of the cooking time. I've found toasting the crumb adds a subtle richness.

SERVES 4
Preparation and cooking time 1½ hours

Preheat the oven to 180°C (160°C fan-forced). Drizzle half of the oil over the pork cubes, mix well and season with a little salt and freshly ground black pepper.

Heat a large flameproof casserole dish over a medium–high heat. Brown the pork in three batches, removing each and reserving as you go; reheat the dish between batches.

Add the remaining oil to the dish, add the onion and cook, stirring, for 1 minute to soften but not brown. Add the garlic and stir for a further 30 seconds. Add the purée, stock, cloves and cinnamon and let the mixture come to the boil. Return the pork to the dish and mix well. Cover the dish and place in the preheated oven. Cook, stirring the pork once or twice, for 1 hour 10 minutes, or until the pork is tender. Remove the cloves.

Meanwhile, make the crumb. Heat the oil in a small frying pan over a medium heat, add the garlic and stir for 10 seconds, then add the crumbs and walnuts and cook, stirring, for 2 minutes, or until the mixture is golden brown. Reserve.

When the pork is tender, stir in half of the toasted crumb mixture. Scatter with parsley leaves and the remaining crumb. Serve immediately.

⅓ cup extra-virgin olive oil
1 kg pork neck or boneless pork shoulder, cut into 3 cm cubes
2 onions, chopped
3 garlic cloves, chopped
1 cup tomato purée
625 ml beef stock
4 cloves
2 teaspoons ground cinnamon
⅓ cup flat-leaf parsley to serve

Garlic walnut crumb
1 tablespoon extra-virgin olive oil
4 garlic cloves, finely chopped
2 slices white bread, processed to crumbs
3 tablespoons finely chopped walnuts

Slow-roasted lamb with salad of black-eyed peas and herbs

Arní sto fórno psiméni árga may saláta mavromátika kai meróudia

I love slow roasting lamb and cooking it on the bone gives it so much more flavour. Ask the butcher to leave the shank bone attached. This is great served with silverbeet pilaf (page 148).

SERVES 4
Preparation and cooking time
3¼–4¼ hours + 10 minutes resting

Preheat the oven to 160°C (140°C fan-forced). Place the lamb in a roasting tin. Combine the oil, vinegar, rigani and fennel. Rub the mixture over the lamb, then sprinkle the lamb with the salt and thyme sprigs and season well with freshly ground black pepper.

Roast the lamb, uncovered, for 3 hours (it will be meltingly tender) or for 4 hours if you want the meat to fall from the bone.

Meanwhile, cook the black-eyed peas for the salad. Place them in a medium saucepan with the garlic and bay leaf. Cover with cold water, place over a medium–low heat and simmer for 50–60 minutes, or until the peas are soft and tender. Drain.

To serve, remove the lamb from the oven, cover loosely with foil and stand for 10 minutes. Toss all of the salad ingredients together and season well with salt and freshly ground black pepper. Use a carving fork and knife to slice or pull the lamb from the bone and serve with the salad.

Lyndey's notes *You could use a shoulder of lamb in place of the leg, if you prefer.*

A can of drained and rinsed butter beans or chickpeas can be used instead of the black-eyed peas.

1.5 kg lamb leg, with shank bone attached (see Lyndey's notes)
½ cup extra-virgin olive oil
¼ cup red wine vinegar
1 tablespoon rigani
1 tablespoon fennel seeds
2 teaspoons sea salt flakes
6 thyme sprigs

Salad of black-eyed peas and herbs
1 cup dried black-eyed peas (see Lyndey's notes)
2 garlic cloves, peeled
1 bay leaf
½ cup sliced sundried tomatoes
2 tablespoons capers, roughly chopped
½ cup pitted kalamata olives, cut into halves
1 cup flat-leaf parsley
2 tablespoons wine vinegar
¼ cup extra-virgin olive oil
100 g feta, crumbled (optional)

Braised green beans and potato

Fasólia sti kasérola me patátas

There are many versions of vegetables braised with tomato. I'd forgotten how good such vegetables can taste.

Heat the oil in a large frying pan (one with a lid) over a medium heat, add the onion and cook, stirring, for 1 minute to soften but not brown the onion. Add the garlic, stir for 30 seconds, then add the tomato paste and stir for a further 1 minute.

Arrange the potatoes in the pan. Add the tomatoes, thyme and water. Add the salt and sugar and season with freshly ground black pepper.

Partially cover the pan with the lid, reduce the heat to low and simmer for 8—10 minutes, or until the potatoes are nearly tender. Add the beans, partially cover the pan again and cook for 3—5 minutes. Remove the lid to evaporate a little of the braising liquid if needed.

Serve warm, drizzled with a little red wine vinegar and extra-virgin olive oil.

Lyndey's note *If you like, add 1 cup of frozen okra or sliced zucchini (courgette) in the last 10 minutes of cooking time.*

| SERVES 4
Preparation and cooking time
35 minutes

¼ cup extra-virgin olive oil
1 large red onion, cut into halves and sliced
3 garlic cloves, chopped
2 tablespoons tomato paste
600 g (3 medium) waxy potatoes, peeled and cut into quarters lengthwise
2 tomatoes, chopped
2 thyme sprigs
1½ cups water
1 teaspoon sea salt flakes
1 teaspoon sugar
300 g young green beans, trimmed and cut in half
red wine vinegar to serve
extra-virgin olive oil to serve

Silverbeet pilaf
Piláfi seskoulo

I was surprised to find how popular rice is in Greece. Pilaf or pilafi is quite richly flavoured and I find myself going back for just one more spoonful!

Trim the silverbeet leaves of their tough white stalks, leaving a little on near the leaf. Wash the leaves, then stack and roll them. Once they are rolled, use a knife to shred the silverbeet.

Place the oil and butter in a deep frying pan (one with a lid) and heat the mixture over a medium heat until the butter has melted and is starting to colour. Add the onion and garlic and cook, stirring, for 1–2 minutes, or until the onion is soft. Add the rice, stir to coat the grains, then add the salt, zest, juice and water and stir to mix. Bring to the boil and cook until the water has evaporated and tunnels begin to form in the rice. Place the silverbeet evenly over the rice and cover the frying pan with the lid. Reduce the heat to low, cook for 10 minutes, and then turn off the heat. Stand for 5 minutes.

To serve, gently stir the rice to distribute the silverbeet. Sprinkle with the dill and green onions.

SERVES 4
Preparation and cooking time
25 minutes + 5 minutes standing

6 silverbeet (Swiss chard) leaves
¼ cup extra-virgin olive oil
20 g butter
1 red onion, finely chopped
2 garlic cloves, finely chopped
1½ cups white long-grain rice
2 teaspoons sea salt flakes
grated zest and juice of 1 lemon
430 ml water
1 cup dill, chopped
2 green onions (shallots), finely chopped

Lentil and chickpea salad

Fákes kai revíthia saláta

Traditionally, dried lentils and chickpeas would be used in a salad like this but using canned pulses saves so much time. Removing the outer skin of the chickpeas gives a lovely result.

Heat the oil in a small frying pan over a medium heat, add the carrot and onion and cook, stirring occasionally for 1–2 minutes, until softened. Add the vinegar and cook for a further 30 seconds until evaporated. Remove from the heat.

Place the chickpeas in a large bowl of water. Gently roll the chickpeas between your palms in the water and the skins will slip away. Skim off the skins then drain the chickpeas.

Place the chickpeas, lentils, carrot and onion mixture, celery, cumin and salt in a large bowl. Season with freshly ground black pepper, then add enough of the extra vinegar and oil to coat the ingredients and to your preferred taste. To serve, add the coriander and parsley and toss to combine.

SERVES 4–6
Preparation and cooking time
15 minutes

- 2 tablespoons extra-virgin olive oil
- 1 small carrot, peeled and finely chopped
- 1 small red onion, finely chopped
- ¼ cup red wine vinegar
- 400 g can chickpeas, drained and rinsed
- 400 g can green lentils, drained and rinsed
- 3 celery stalks, strung, sliced diagonally
- 2 teaspoons ground cumin
- 2 teaspoons sea salt flakes
- red wine vinegar and extra-virgin olive oil, extra, to taste
- ½ bunch coriander leaves
- ½ bunch flat-leaf parsley

Diples

Diples

Dimitris' mother, Penelope, invited me to make these at her house in Stoupa with another two ladies. Diples are made in very large quantities in Greece and offered at celebrations, such as weddings, baptisms, the opening of a new shop or moving house. Women always work in groups when they can be making upward of 300 or more. They keep in an airtight tin for months. This recipe makes more manageable quantities.

Whisk the eggs vigorously until pale. Add the sugar and continue whisking until the sugar is dissolved. Slowly add the flour, whisking constantly until a dough forms. Oil your hands and knead the dough until smooth. Wrap in plastic wrap and rest for 30 minutes.

Divide the dough into several balls. Roll each piece until thin or else use a pasta machine up to its finest or second finest setting. To test if it is thin enough, lift a corner of the dough and gently blow under it — it should lift. If not, roll thinner and test again.

Using a serrated pastry cutter, cut the dough into 4 x 50 cm strips. Pinch the two sides of each strip together at 2–3cm intervals making little pockets as you go. Pull the strip around on itself, into a spiral, squeezing together to hold in place and make firm. They will look like frilly rosettes.

Pour oil into a medium heavy-based saucepan to a depth of about 10 cm and place over a medium–high heat. Test the heat of the oil with a wooden implement to see if bubbles appear.

Drop the prepared rosette diples in the pan a couple at a time and cook until a light golden colour, rolling over to cook both sides. Drain on paper towels.

Cook the syrup ingredients until hot. Dip the diples in the hot syrup, making sure they are completely coated. Drain.

Serve the diples dusted with ground walnuts and cinnamon and garnished with sugared almonds and edible flowers.

Lyndey's note *A much simpler way is to roll the dough out the width of a pasta machine (about 13 cm) and then cut into lengths of around 12 cm. Hold one edge with tongs and place in the hot oil. As they start to puff, roll into cylinder shapes. This can be done with another pair of tongs or in Greece they use a long carving fork and a spatula.*

MAKES 15–20
Preparation and cooking time
45 minutes + 30 minutes resting

3 eggs
¼ cup sugar
2 cups plain flour
1 tablespoon oil to oil hands
extra-virgin olive oil for deep-frying

Honey syrup
1 cup honey
1 cup sugar
3 teaspoons orange juice
½ cup water
½ cinnamon stick
2 cloves

To serve
ground walnuts
ground cinnamon
sugared almonds
edible flowers (optional)

CAPE TENARO AND HADES

Tales of Hades are the stuff of myth and legend with the idea of a never-ending descent into the 'dark world beyond'. We wanted to see it for ourselves and made our way down to the southerly most point of Europe to find it. There a pebbly little beach adjoins another little cove, with the tiniest little cave tucked away in the rocks. This is reputed to be the entrance to the underworld! While it was a bit of an anticlimax we learned later that this 'tiny' little entrance indeed must have been massive in ancient times but earthquakes and land subsidence have taken their toll.

Greek creamed rice
Rizógalos

This recipe has completely changed my mind about rice pudding. Using lots of liquid makes for a creamy, appetising result. It is delicious with poached quinces with orange flower water (page 101).

Combine the milk, sugar and orange zest in a medium saucepan, place over a medium heat and bring to the boil, stirring occasionally.

Gradually stir in the rice. Reduce the heat to low, add the cinnamon stick, cover the pan and cook, stirring occasionally, for about 40 minutes, or until the rice is tender. Remove the cinnamon stick and orange zest.

Meanwhile, blend the cornflour and the extra 2 teaspoons milk to a smooth paste in a small bowl, then stir in the egg yolks. Pour the hot milk over the egg mixture, whisking well to combine. Pour into the rice, stirring over low heat until the mixture thickens. Stir in the vanilla.

Pour into individual bowls. Serve warm or cooled, sprinkled with walnuts, cinnamon sugar and honey.

Lyndey's note *This recipe can be made a day ahead.*

SERVES 4
Preparation and cooking time
1 hour

1 litre milk
⅓ cup caster sugar
1 large strip orange zest
⅓ cup white medium-grain rice
1 cinnamon stick
2 teaspoons cornflour
2 teaspoons milk, extra
4 egg yolks, lightly beaten
¼ cup milk, extra, hot
½ teaspoon vanilla essence
¼ cup walnut pieces, toasted
¼ teaspoon ground cinnamon mixed with ¼ teaspoon caster sugar
1 tablespoon honey

Garídes kai ostráka may kataïfi may kaftéri pipéria skordália ~ Haloúmi may máratho portókali kai elíes Kalámon ~ Souvláki may skordália ~ Arní fricassee ~ Kokára e kotópolo krassáto me hóndres patátes ~ Okra lathéra ~ Kourambíedes ~ Karídia portókali kai eliólado kaik me sirópi ~ Loukóumádes me sirópi tou melíou ~ Yemísta filópita me karídia, stafídia síka kai diósmos

Chapter 6
Kalamata, Messene and Outer Mani

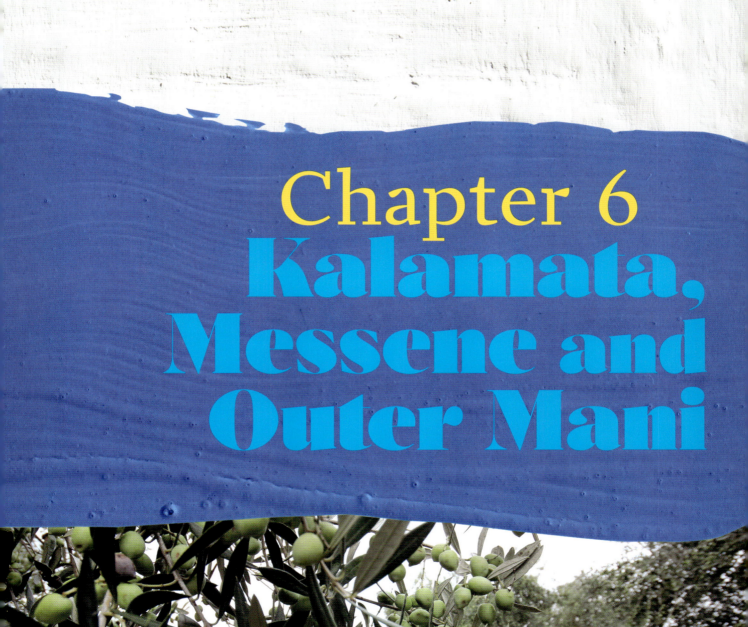

Blair and I love markets.

Always have, especially when there is terrific regional food on offer. It's one of the joys of travelling. We were in our element as we explored the outdoor and covered market in Kalamata seeing only fresh regional produce and applauding that this is the way Greeks cook. If it isn't in season, they don't use it. We tried everything we could from souvlaki sticks fresh off the charcoal crammed into a bread roll, chunky local sausage spiked with orange and Blair was especially excited to eat the delicious kalamata olives right there in Kalamata. We finished off with piping hot loukoumades deep-fried in olive oil and if that sweet treat wasn't enough, we managed to eat some of the indulgent chocolate-covered figs of the area.

We were fascinated by the hive of activity and the attention to detail that went into producing first-class olive oil and figs at a local factory.

Our next injection of history was the archaeological site of Ancient Messene. What a wonder! A purpose-built city, so well preserved and complete with a stadium and a small amphitheatre that Blair longed to perform in. Later I was to cook and then we dined at Ithomi Restaurant overlooking the site. I'd never cooked cockerel (or rooster) before and the okra was so tender and sweet. Blair and I were lost for words as we tucked in overlooking one of the wonders of the Peloponnese.

The next day we made our way to the dramatic Methoni castle once occupied by the Venetians and on our long journey to our next location, stopped to challenge a local to a game of tavli (backgammon). Guess who won?

Prawns and scallops in kataifi with spicy capsicum skordalia

Garídes kai ostráka may kataïfi may kaftéri pipéria skordália

Kataifi pastry is made with a special form of shredded filo dough. It is usually used in sweets, especially those with nuts and honey but I also like it in savoury dishes. With patience you can make your own by shredding filo into very fine strips.

Open the packet of kataifi pastry, place in a bowl and loosen the strands with your fingers. Return half of the pastry to the packet for later use.

Add the melted butter and dill to the pastry in the bowl, then mix with your fingers until the pastry is evenly coated. Place about 1 tablespoon of the pastry on a board and gently stretch to form a 10 cm long strip. Place a prawn at one end of the strip and roll the pastry around the prawn. Place on a tray. Continue with the remaining prawns. Repeat the process with the scallops. Cover with a clean tea towel to prevent drying out; refrigerate until needed.

To make the skordalia, blitz the chilli, bread and salt in a food processor until crumbs form. Add the capsicum and process again until smooth. While the food processor is working, add the vinegar and then slowly add the oil until the mixture blends to a smooth, creamy texture.

Heat the oil in a large frying pan over a medium–high heat and cook the prawns and scallops in batches, the prawns for 2 minutes on each side and the scallops for 1–2 minutes on each side, or until golden and cooked through (reduce the heat to medium if they are cooking too quickly). Reheat the oil between batches. Drain on paper towels.

Serve the fried prawns and scallops with the skordalia.

Lyndey's note *The prawns and scallops can be prepared ahead of time: wrap them in the kataifi pastry, place on a tray in a single layer, cover and keep in the refrigerator for up to 3–4 hours. The spicy capsicum skordalia can be made several days ahead.*

SERVES 6–8 as part of a meze
Preparation and cooking time
30 minutes

½ × 375 g packet of kataifi pastry
90 g butter, melted
½ cup chopped dill
12 large raw prawns, peeled and deveined with tails intact
12 large fresh scallops
½ cup extra-virgin olive oil

Spicy capsicum skordalia
1 long mild red chilli, deseeded and roughly chopped
2 slices white bread, crusts removed
1 teaspoon sea salt flakes
250 g roasted red capsicums in oil, drained
1 tablespoon red wine vinegar
¼ cup extra-virgin olive oil

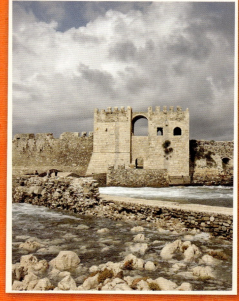

METHONI

There's something very dramatic about the fortress of Methoni: those who want entry must first cross a stone bridge over a very impressive moat. Built by the Venetians, the fortress was once a stopover for pilgrims and traders on their way to the Holy Land. A bridge with waves crashing over it links the fortress to a small island citadel with an extraordinary eight-sided tower where prisoners were once held. Locals say that when the wind is in the right direction and the sea is crashing you can still hear the screams of those prisoners. This citadel is also the place where the Venetians made their last stand against the Turks in 1500, retreating to the citadel where they met their end.

Some say that the pretty town of Methoni got its name from the fact that donkeys (onoi) transported the town's wine and became drunk (methoun) — hence Methoni. I'm not sure about that but even Homer mentions that the area was 'rich in vines'.

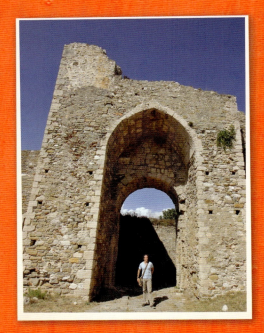

Haloumi with fennel, orange and kalamata olives

Haloúmi may máratho portókali kai elíes Kalámon

This brings together some of the things we saw in the Kalamata market in a modern interpretation.

SERVES 4 as part of a meze
Preparation and cooking time 15 minutes

2 oranges
3 baby fennel bulbs or 1 medium bulb
350 g haloumi
2 tablespoons extra-virgin olive oil
1 small red onion, cut into halves and finely sliced
½ cup pitted kalamata olives, cut into halves

Use a small sharp knife to remove the skin and pith of the oranges, following the curves of the oranges to slice the skin and pith away. Cut the oranges between the flesh and the membrane to remove the segments — do this over a small bowl to catch the juice, and then squeeze any juice from the membrane. Reserve.

Remove the base and cut the stalks from the fennel bulbs, halve the bulbs and remove the core. Cut the fennel into thin wedges. Reserve.

Preheat a frying pan over medium–high heat. Working from the narrowest width of the haloumi, cut it into 1.5 cm thick slices, then brush with a little oil. Cook for 2 minutes on each side, or until golden. Place the haloumi on a serving platter.

Toss the orange segments, onion, fennel and olives together. Place over the haloumi, drizzle with the orange juice and remaining oil and season to taste with salt and freshly ground black pepper.

Souvlaki with skordalia
Souvláki may skordália

Souvlaki is the term used to describe 'little skewers' of meat, usually pork, that are marinated then grilled over a charcoal burner — common all over Greece. Delicious on their own, they may be wrapped in any type of bread and are served just as they are as the ultimate fast food. You can add a sauce, perhaps skordalia, tzatziki or even homemade tomato sauce. The meat is best marinated for 2–3 hours to really absorb the flavours. Skordalia is not traditionally served with souvlaki but I love this garlic sauce. It's often made with potato but I like the bread-based version best.

To make the skordalia, briefly soak the bread in enough cold water to cover, then squeeze out well. Chop the garlic in a food processor, then add the bread and lemon juice. Slowly drizzle in the oil and then the water until the mixture is smooth and has a texture similar to white sauce. If it is too thick, add more water, 1 teaspoon at a time. Season to taste with salt, freshly ground black pepper and lemon juice.

To make the marinade, whisk the marinade ingredients together in a large bowl. Add the pork cubes, cover and refrigerate for 2–3 hours. If using wooden skewers, soak these in water or freeze while the meat marinates. Thread the pork on to the skewers (about six pieces per skewer). Season the pork with salt and freshly ground black pepper. Heat the grill, barbecue or hotplate to medium–high.

Grill the souvlaki for a few minutes on each side, turning once or twice until they are cooked through.

Serve immediately, with a squeeze of lemon juice, the skordalia and pita bread, if you like.

Lyndey's note *If you are serving the souvlaki with pita, it can be toasted on the grill too.*

SERVES 4
Preparation and cooking time
25 minutes + 2–3 hours marinating

600 g pork neck or shoulder, cut into 2 cm cubes
lemon to serve
pita bread to serve (optional) (see Lyndey's note)

Garlic marinade
¼ cup extra-virgin olive oil
juice of 1 large lemon
2 teaspoons dried mint
1 tablespoon rigani
4 garlic cloves, finely chopped

Skordalia
⅓ loaf (100 g) strong white bread (e.g. sourdough), crust removed
2 garlic cloves
1–2 teaspoons lemon juice, or to taste
⅓ cup extra-virgin olive oil
about ⅓ cup water
lemon juice to taste

Greek olive oil and olives

Nowhere is oil loved and revered more than in Greece. It has been the most significant ingredient in the Greek diet since ancient times and is still an integral part of the Greek kitchen and rightfully celebrated on Greek tables. For Greeks cannot eat without oil. Rich, flavoursome extra-virgin olive oil is on the table at all meals: bread is dipped in it; salads and vegetables are doused with it; it is poured over soups, stews and many other dishes.

Oil is used liberally in cooking, sometimes a surprising amount is called for. 'Close your eyes and add oil' is the wisdom imparted by many older Greek cooks (what this means is that a good amount of oil should be added). The Greeks even have a word for dishes prepared with lots of oil: ladera (from the Greek word for oil, ladi).

The recipe for okra ladera (page 170) is a good example of the dishes made with a generous amount of oil. Use the amount listed in the recipes or your meal won't have that authentic Greek flavour. Extra-virgin olive oil completely changes not only the taste but also the texture and richness of many favourite dishes.

The interesting thing is in Greece, the oil is virtually all extra-virgin olive oil. New season's oil is used at the table, for salads and to pour over finished dishes while last season's is used for cooking and deep-frying. And what a wonderful medium it is for deep-frying!

Greeks consume more oil per capita than any other nation in the world, an average of 26 litres per person, per year! Despite its relatively small size Greece is the third largest producer of oil (behind Spain and Italy), with around 140 million olive trees, which produce approximately 450,000 tons of olives a year, 80 per cent of which is extra-virgin olive oil, making Greece the world leader in this oil.

In the Peloponnese, olive trees thrive (the region accounts for roughly 65 per cent of Greece's annual oil production), producing extra-virgin olive oil of exceptional quality and flavour. Most Greek oil is extracted from the Koroneiki, which produce oil with a full-bodied, robust, yet balanced flavour.

Greek extra-virgin olive oils are often described as herbaceous or grassy in character, with notable olive fruitiness or pepperiness. Look out for oil labelled as agourelaio, it is considered the best of the best. It is pressed from the first olives harvested that are green and not very ripe. It will be deep golden green in colour, fresh and very fruity.

TABLE OLIVES

Sharing olives and bread is a mark of friendship in Greece. It was very common in years gone by for olives to be served with a glass of ouzo as prosfagio (the word for a bite before your meal to encourage your appetite) before meze dishes are served.

Olives are not common in traditional Greek cooking, but they are included in some tomato-based sauces and are used to flavour fillings for pies and pastries and are used in some breads. They are an important ingredient in Greek salad. Today they are used in many innovative ways in modern Greek cuisine.

Most people recognise Greek olives by their place name or by the way they have been cured. Kalamata olives are undoubtedly the most recognisable Greek olive, with their deep purple colour and slightly pointed end and rich and fruity flavour. They are often slit so the curing brine gets well into the flesh.

Within Greece, the most familiar variety of olive is the conserviola. Large and oval, these are harvested at varying stages from dark green, greenish-yellow, pinkish-brown to black. These taste a little salty, with a red wine flavour and a slightly bitter finish. They're softer in texture than other Greek olives and more loosely attached to the stone. Several versions of this olive have been accorded Protected Designation of Origin Status.

Fleshy halkidiki olives are pale green in colour (outside of Greece they are mostly sold as large green Greek olives). They are grown in the region around Thessaloniki and are exported all over the world. They are a very pleasant olive to nibble, firm with a yielding bite. They are the most common Greek olive to stuff.

Megaritiki olives are grown in Attica, near Athens. These are cracked, brined and packed with lemon slices.

The black, wrinkly Greek olives often seen in delicatessens are called throubes (dry olives). Originating on the island of Thassos, these olives are harvested when very ripe, sundried and then lightly salted and packed in oil. In Australia they are sold as Thassos olives. They have a very meaty olive flavour.

Lamb fricassee

Arni fricassee

Fricassee is really just a stew, typically made with poultry though other meats can also be used. It is thickened with butter, cream or milk. Greek fricassee is often made with lamb and usually contains lettuce and/or wild herbs; the gravy is thickened with beaten eggs just before serving.

Drizzle half of the oil over the lamb cubes, mix well and season with a little salt and freshly ground black pepper. Heat a large flameproof casserole dish (one with a lid) over a medium–high heat. Brown the lamb in three batches, reheating the dish between batches.

Heat the remaining oil in the dish, add the onion and cook, stirring, for 1 minute to soften but not brown the onion. Add the garlic and stir for a further 30 seconds. Add the green onions, celery, dill and the browned lamb to the dish. Stir to mix, then add the lettuce — it will look like it won't all fit, but stir two or three times to soften lettuce, this can take a few minutes.

Reduce the heat to low and add enough water to just cover the lamb mixture. Cover the dish with the lid and simmer gently, stirring once or twice, for 1½ hours, or until the lamb is tender.

Towards the end of the cooking time, whisk together the eggs, lemon juice and yoghurt, if using. Set aside until needed.

Once the lamb is tender when tested with a fork and you are ready to serve, take a ladleful of the cooking liquid from the dish and whisk it into the egg and lemon juice mixture. Pour the mixture into the dish, stirring it through and continue to stir over a low heat until the sauce thickens slightly; do not let it boil. Serve immediately. Sprinkle with extra chopped dill, if you like.

SERVES 4
Preparation and cooking time
2 hours

- ⅓ cup extra-virgin olive oil
- 1.5 kg leg of lamb, boned, cut into 3 cm cubes
- 1 red onion, chopped
- 3 garlic cloves, chopped
- 4 green onions (shallots), finely chopped
- 2 small celery stalks, finely diced
- ¼–½ bunch dill (leaves and tender stalks), chopped
- 1 cos (romaine) lettuce, washed, shredded
- 2 eggs
- juice of 1 small lemon
- 1 tablespoon Greek-style natural yoghurt (optional)
- chopped dill, extra, to serve (optional)

ANCIENT MESSENE

We were bowled over by this little visited but impressive site. What is amazing is that this is a purpose-built city, not one which grew organically. In 371 BC, Epaminondas defeated the Spartans and liberated the Messenians who had been in servitude to the Spartans for over 300 years. Epaminondas built this city, complete with city wall in 369 BC to keep the Spartans out. The city has over 9 kilometres of walls up to 10 metres high and was immediately occupied by the Messenian people. It remains in astonishing condition to this day. Blair couldn't resist climbing the grand Arcadian gate and then we wandered around at will through the site with its theatre, stadium with newly restored seating, temples, students' changing rooms, central market and private homes. It is still being excavated and promises to become one of the most important archaeological sites in the Peloponnese.

Cockerel or chicken in wine with potatoes

Kokára e kotópolo krassáto me hóndres patátes

Cockerel is rooster, but the recipe could also be made with a large free-range chicken. At Ithomi restaurant, it clearly wasn't too old. Rooster, being older and tougher, will need longer, slower cooking than a chicken.

Joint the cockerel or chicken into six pieces, known as 'country-style' in Greece.

Heat the oil over a medium heat in a large frying pan until hot. Add the onion and cockerel or chicken pieces, seasoning with salt and freshly ground black pepper as they go in. Cook for about 15 minutes, turning until golden brown all over. Discard the onion.

Place the cockerel or chicken and a couple of spoonfuls of the oil from the frying pan in a large flameproof casserole dish (one with a lid). Place over a medium heat, add the wine and boil to evaporate off the alcohol. Add enough water to almost cover the cockerel or chicken. Bring to the boil, cover with the lid and reduce the heat to low.

If you are using chicken, cook it for 35–40 minutes, or until tender. If you are using cockerel, cook for 1¼ hours and, if still not tender, place in a preheated (180°C/160°C fan-forced) oven for a further 1¼ hours, or until tender. Taste and adjust the seasoning if necessary.

Pour plenty of the extra oil into a medium heavy-based saucepan and place over a medium–high heat. Test the heat of the oil with a wooden implement to see if bubbles appear. Deep-fry potatoes in batches until golden and tender, up to 8–10 minutes per batch.

Remove the lid from the cockerel or chicken and lay the potatoes on the top of the dish. Sprinkle with rigani, if using, then serve.

Lyndey's note *If preparing in advance, as is often done in Greece, place the potatoes on top and return the covered pan to the oven to keep warm until serving time.*

SERVES 6
Preparation and cooking time
3 hours for cockerel or 1¼ hours for chicken

- 2.4 kg cockerel or 2 kg free-range chicken
- ¾ cup extra-virgin olive oil
- 1 small red onion, cut into quarters
- ⅔ cup white wine
- extra-virgin olive oil, extra, for deep-frying
- 1.2 kg (about 6) potatoes, peeled, thickly sliced and patted dry
- rigani (optional)

Okra ladera

Okra lathéra

This was cooked at Ithomi restaurant overlooking Ancient Messene. Stavroula, the cook and restaurant owner's mother, deep-fries her okra first and explained that this stops the okra going mucilaginous as it usually does when cooked. I've tried it and it really does work.

To make the sauce, blend the tomatoes in a blender until smooth. Heat the oil in a large frying pan over a medium heat. Add the onions and garlic and cook until the onions are soft but not brown. Add the tomatoes, salt, sugar and some freshly ground black pepper and cook, stirring occasionally for 10–15 minutes, or until the sauce thickens slightly.

Preheat the oven to 180°C (160°C fan-forced). Pour plenty of oil into a medium heavy-based saucepan and place over a medium–high heat. Test the heat of the oil with a wooden implement to see if bubbles appear.

Wash the okra and remove the stalk or top ends, then place on paper towels to dry.

Deep-fry the okra in batches until the colour heightens, about 2–3 minutes per batch. Drain on paper towels.

Place half the tomato sauce in a large baking dish. Cover with the okra and then spoon the remaining tomato sauce over the okra, spreading it over the top. Bake, uncovered, for 20–30 minutes, or until thoroughly hot. A longer cooking time reduces and intensifies the tomato sauce.

Lyndey's note You can substitute the fresh tomato sauce with 2 cups canned tomatoes or tomato purée, if you prefer.

SERVES 8 as a side dish
Preparation and cooking time
1 hour

extra-virgin olive oil for deep-frying
1 kg fresh young okra

Tomato sauce
1 kg ripe tomatoes, peeled, deseeded and chopped (see Lyndey's note)
⅓ cup olive oil
2 large red onions, finely chopped
2 garlic cloves, chopped
1 teaspoon sea salt flakes
1 teaspoon sugar

Easter in Greece

'Kalo Pascha' — 'Have a good Easter'. The Easter season is a special one in Greece with many foods and traditions marking the season as uniquely Hellenic. Even the date is different from Christian Easter as Greek Orthodox Easter is based on the Julian rather than Gregorian calendar.

Before the Lenten fast begins, there is the Carnival or Apokries season, which runs for the three weeks preceding Lent. This is a period of good eating and drinking before the clean living of Lent begins. The period includes Burnt Thursday, which refers to the grilling of meat and it is a day when tavernas are jammed full of families eating their fill before fasting begins.

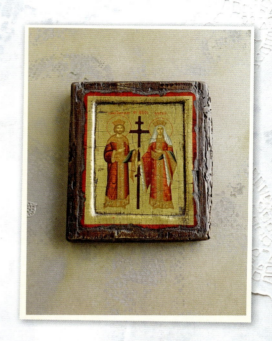

The Easter season starts on Kathará Deftéra (Clean Monday), forty days before Easter. From that day until Easter Sunday nothing can be eaten with blood flowing through its veins.

During the last week before Easter, Holy Week, fasting is stricter and even olive oil is not consumed — the religious eat only vegetables and bread. The Thursday before Easter, Holy Thursday, is the day when Kokina Paschalina avga, the bright dyed red eggs symbolic of Easter in Greece are prepared. The eggs are then set aside until Easter Sunday when they become part of a traditional Easter game: each person takes an egg and challengers attempt to crack each other's eggs. The person whose egg lasts the longest is assured good luck for the rest of the year.

Late at night on Good Friday the Epitafios or tomb of Christ, smothered in fresh flowers, is taken through the village, which is lit up by onlookers holding candles.

Holy Saturday is a day of excited preparation. At midnight the church bells toll to symbolise the Resurrection as the priests announce, 'Christós anésti!' ('Christ is Risen!'). After church, in most areas of Greece, magaritsa soup and some bread are eaten.

Next day is a wonderful feast of indulgence that comprises food that has been given up for Lent: lamb or goat on the spit, salads of beans, greens and seafood, cheese pies, vegetable dishes, cakes, sweets and plenty of wine. The celebration continues all day and night and anything left over is eaten on Easter Monday.

Easter bread *Tsoureki*

MAKES 1 loaf **Preparation and cooking time** 1 hour 20 minutes + 2 hours 45 minutes proving

---

Place 1 cup milk in a bowl, sprinkle in 2 teaspoons (7 g) dried yeast and 1 teaspoon caster sugar and whisk until the yeast is dissolved. Stir in ½ cup sifted flour, cover and stand in a warm place for 30 minutes, or until the mixture has doubled.

Stir in 150 g melted butter, 2 lightly beaten eggs, the finely grated zest of 1 orange, 2 teaspoons aniseed (or 2 teaspoons mahlepi and ½ teaspoon masticha), ½ teaspoon salt and a further ⅓ cup caster sugar, then gradually stir in a further 3 cups sifted plain flour to form a dough. Gently knead the dough on a floured surface for about 10 minutes, or until smooth and elastic. Lightly oil a large bowl, place the dough in the bowl, cover and stand in a warm place until doubled in size (about 1½ hours).

Turn out and knead for 1–2 minutes. Cut the dough into three even pieces and roll each piece into a 40 cm long cylinder, plait the lengths together, then shape into a wreath, pinching the ends to join. Place on a lined baking tray. Press 3 red eggs firmly into the wreath. Stand in a warm place until well risen (about 45 minutes).

Preheat the oven to 200°C (180°C fan-forced). Brush the bread with a combined egg yolk and 2 tablespoons milk, then bake for 10 minutes. Reduce the heat to 180°C (160°C fan-forced) and bake for a further 30 minutes, or until the bread sounds hollow when tapped.

Lyndey's note *This bread is part of the traditional midnight supper early on Easter Sunday morning after the Resurrection Service. The three dough ropes plaited together symbolise the Holy Trinity; the red eggs symbolise the blood shed by Christ. It is best made on the day of serving. It is delicious toasted after that.*

Red eggs *Kokina Paschalina avga*

Measure 1 cup warm water and ½ cup white vinegar in a glass jug, add 1 sachet Greek red food dye (see Lyndey's note) and mix well. Fill a large saucepan with 1.75 litres warm water, add the dye mix, stir well. Gently place 12 eggs in a single layer into the saucepan. Bring to the boil, reduce the heat, simmer, uncovered, for 15 minutes. Gently remove the eggs and cool. Polish the eggs with a lightly oiled cloth before using.

Lyndey's note *1 sachet of Greek red food dye will colour 1 dozen eggs. It is available from Greek delicatessens and some supermarket deli counters. Take care as the dye is strong and will stain. A strong gel or powdered food colour can also be used, but liquid food colours don't give an intense colour. Make sure the eggs are not crowded in the pan as they cook, or they will not colour evenly.*

From left: Red eggs, Easter bread.

Greek shortbread cookies
Kourambiedes

Crumbly, soft appealing shortbread is one of the cornerstones of Greek baking. I never tire of it.

MAKES about 40
Preparation and cooking time
50 minutes

250 g unsalted butter, softened
⅔ cup icing sugar
1 teaspoon finely grated orange zest (see Lyndey's note)
1 egg yolk
1 tablespoon ouzo or brandy
¾ cup ground almonds
2½ cups self-raising flour
1 cup icing sugar, extra

Preheat the oven to 180°C (160°C fan-forced). Line two baking trays with baking paper.

Beat the butter, icing sugar and orange zest in a bowl with electric beaters until light and creamy. Add the egg yolk and ouzo and beat until well combined. Add the almonds and flour and mix on low speed to form a soft dough.

Shape level tablespoons of the mixture into crescent shapes. Place 3 cm apart on the prepared trays.

Bake for 12–15 minutes, or until lightly golden. Stand for 3–5 minutes before transferring to a wire rack to cool. While still warm, sift over half of the extra icing sugar. Turn the biscuits over and sift over remaining icing sugar to coat completely. Cool.

Store in an airtight container for up to 1 week.

Lyndey's note *Replace the orange zest with vanilla essence, if you like. The biscuits can also be sprinkled with a little rosewater while still warm, before dusting with icing sugar.*

Walnut, orange and olive oil cake with spice syrup

Karídia portókali kai eliólado kaik me sirópi

There are many versions of walnut cake throughout the Mediterranean. The addition of orange and a spice syrup gives this one an extra dimension.

Preheat the oven to 180°C (160°C fan-forced). Grease the base and sides of a non-stick 23 cm square cake tin.

Using electric beaters, beat the eggs in a medium bowl until thick and creamy, then gradually add the caster sugar and beat well after each addition. Add the orange zest and juice and beat until well combined. Slowly add the oil, beating until well combined.

Fold in the flour, ground cinnamon and walnuts. Pour the cake batter into the tin. Bake for 30–35 minutes.

Meanwhile, to make the syrup, combine the water, sugar, orange zest, cloves and cinnamon sticks in a medium saucepan and cook over a medium heat until the sugar has dissolved. Bring to the boil, reduce the heat to low and simmer for 5 minutes. Remove the cloves and cinnamon.

When the cake is cooked, leave it in the tin for 5 minutes before turning the cake onto a wire rack over a tray; leave it upside down. Using a fine skewer, gently pierce holes randomly over the surface of the cake, then pour the hot syrup over it.

Serve the cake warm or cold with a dollop of yoghurt. Store in an airtight container for up to 3 days.

SERVES 8
Preparation and cooking time 50 minutes

3 eggs
¾ cup caster sugar
grated zest and juice of 1 orange
¾ cup olive oil
1 cup self-raising flour
3 teaspoons ground cinnamon
¾ cup chopped walnuts
Greek-style yoghurt to serve

Spice syrup
1 cup water
¾ cup sugar
grated zest of 1 orange
4 cloves
2 cinnamon sticks, halved

GREEK COFFEE

Greek coffee is about much more than making a cup of coffee; it is an important ritual and conversation starter. It's a prelude to business deals and is drunk after funerals, first thing in the morning and straight after siesta.

Greek coffee is strong and thick and can be an acquired taste. You can have it skétos (bitter), métrios (medium sweet) or glíkos (sweet). Traditionally, it is made in a briki, a small pot with a wide bottom, narrow top and a long handle. Combine a teaspoon of very finely ground Greek coffee with a teaspoon of sugar (quantities depend on how strong and how sweet you like it) in a briki with an espresso cup of water. Stir the coffee continuously until it begins to froth but don't allow it to boil. Carefully pour the coffee into an espresso or demitasse cup, leaving behind as many of the coffee grounds as possible. Serve with a glass of ice-cold water and perhaps some confectionery. It is best to let the coffee settle for a few minutes before drinking, then sip it deliberately and slowly to leave the sediment at the bottom of the cup.

For a refreshing change to Greek coffee, try a frappé. Combine a teaspoon of instant coffee, sugar to taste and a quarter of a cup of ice-cold water. Shake or blend the mixture until it foams. Pour into a glass, add a few ice cubes and top up with cold water or milk to taste.

Filo rolls with manouri, walnuts, raisins, figs and mint

Yemísta filópita me karídia, stafídia síka kai diósmos

Again I am using many of the ingredients we saw in Kalamata market in a modern but nonetheless Greek way.

If the filo is frozen, remove it from the freezer and place in the refrigerator the day before it is needed. Cover the filo with baking paper or a dry tea towel, then a damp tea towel to prevent the filo from drying out.

Preheat the oven to 180°C (160°C fan-forced). Line two baking trays with baking paper. Combine the melted butter and oil in a small jug. Drain the soaked raisins and figs, then chop.

Combine the chopped raisins and figs, cheese, mint, walnuts and egg, mix well.

Take one sheet of filo and brush it with a little of the buttery oil mixture, then top with another sheet, again brushing the top with a little more of the buttery oil.

Cut the sheets into three strips widthwise. Place a rounded tablespoon of the cheese mixture at one end, then roll the filo over the filling to enclose. Fold the ends in towards the filling, roll to the end of the strip. Place the roll, seam side down, on a baking tray. Repeat the procedure with the remaining filo and cheese filling.

Brush the rolls with the remaining buttery oil. Bake for 15–20 minutes, or until the pastry is puffed and golden. Stand for 5 minutes before serving.

Lyndey's note Manouri is a semi-soft sheep's or goat's cheese often made from the whey left over from the production of feta. It is mild, slightly sweet and utterly delicious. It is available from Greek delicatessens. Italian-style ricotta salata can be substituted — it's little saltier, but goes well with the dried fruit and walnuts in this recipe.

MAKES 18 rolls
Preparation and cooking time
45 minutes

12 sheets filo
40 g butter, melted
2 tablespoons extra-virgin olive oil
½ cup raisins, soaked in sweet wine or warm water
100 g dried figs, soaked in sweet wine or warm water
250 g manouri cheese or ricotta salata, grated (see Lyndey's note)
¾ cup mint leaves, chopped
½ cup walnut pieces, chopped
1 egg, lightly beaten

Loukoumades with honey syrup

Loukoúmádes me sirópi tou melíou

These are really deep-fried doughnut balls. Freshly cooked they make a popular day time snack with Greek coffee, much as we enjoyed in Kalamata market.

SERVES 6 or MAKES 20
Preparation and cooking time 25 minutes + 1 hour 20 minutes standing

1½ teaspoons dried yeast
1 teaspoon sugar
½ cup warm water
2 cups plain flour
½ teaspoon salt
½ cup milk
extra-virgin olive oil for deep-frying
cinnamon sugar (1 tablespoon ground cinnamon to 1 teaspoon caster sugar) to serve (see Lyndey's note)

Honey syrup
1 cup honey
1 cup sugar
½ cup water

Combine the yeast, sugar and warm water, mix well, cover and stand for 20 minutes, or until frothy. Combine the flour and salt in a large bowl and set it aside. Measure the milk and allow to stand at room temperature.

Add the milk to the yeast mixture, stir to combine and then pour into the flour mixture. Mix well, cover and stand in a warm place for 1 hour, or until doubled in volume.

Meanwhile, to make the syrup, place the honey, sugar and water in a large saucepan and cook over a low heat until hot. Simmer to reduce and thicken a little. Reheat to hot to serve with the loukoumades.

Once the yeast mixture has doubled, stir it well to mix.

Pour oil into a medium heavy-based saucepan to a depth of about 7 cm and place over a medium–high heat. Test the heat of the oil with a wooden implement to see if bubbles appear.

Using two dessertspoons (dip them in oil first), carefully lower spoonfuls of the batter into the hot oil. Do not make them too big or the loukoumades will be doughy in the centre. Cook in batches of about four for 3–4 minutes, or until golden and puffed. Reheat the oil between each batch.

Drain on paper towels. Dip the loukoumades in the hot syrup, rolling them over to make sure they are completely coated. Sprinkle with cinnamon sugar, or just cinnamon if you prefer, and serve immediately.

Lyndey's note Cinnamon sugar is usually equal parts of cinnamon and sugar, but as these are so sweet, it is better to reduce the ratio of sugar.

HONEY

Honey has a special resonance with the Greeks. It is one of the oldest and most legendary foods in Greece and there are many myths associated with it in Greek literature. Legend has it that the mighty Zeus was partly raised on honey and the Greek word for honey, meli, was found inscribed on the famous Linear B tablets from 3500 years ago in Minoan Crete. Concrete evidence of beekeeping was discovered when excavations of a town buried by a volcanic eruption in 1600 BC unearthed the remains of a beehive. Aristotle's zoological writings contain detailed descriptions of how the flavour of honey depends on the flowers the bees visit.

The job of a beekeeper is a highly regarded profession in Greece where the bees feed on unique varieties of trees, flowers and aromatic herbs with thyme honey being the most famous. Because Greece's vegetation is sparser than in some other parts of the world, the bees must work harder and so collecting nectar from a wider variety of plants they produce a honey that is denser and richer in aromatic substances.

Elíes marinates may maratho kai lemóni ~ Piperíes yemísta may tíri ~ Kleftíko ~ Kounéli stifádo ~ Arní yemísto may trachánas kai stafília tou krassíou ~ Souvláki ksiféas may capári kai aníthos ~ Kotópolo yemísto may ginginares maratho kai liástres tomátes ~ Sinagrída may cróusta karídia kai lemóni ródi sirópi ~ Moschári sti kaseróla may melitzána puráys ~ Kounéli krassáto may dentrolívano kai skórdo ~ Oúzo fráppe ~ Tirópitákia

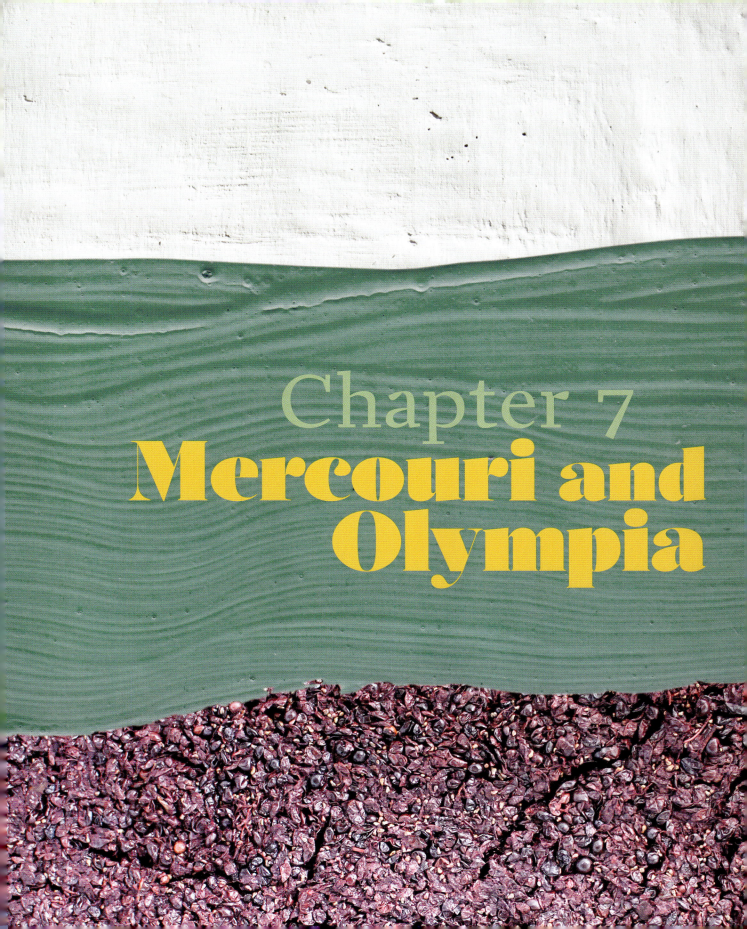

Chapter 7
Mercouri and Olympia

Our *filming in the area of Olympia*

had a wonderful sense of calm and style about it beginning with our visit to the wine estate of Mercouri. The Italianate buildings on the estate came right out of a film and were packed with antiquities. Peacocks, considered very lucky in Greece, strutted about. Our host, Vasilis, was a gentleman with a passion for his heritage in making high-quality wines and olive oil. No wonder I was inspired. The wines were perfectly suited to the lamb dish I intended to cook. Blair and I could have stayed there all day tasting, eating and learning about the wine and olives. However, we had an appointment with the gods at Ancient Olympia, one of the best known sites in the Peloponnese and deservedly so. What we loved so much was that some of the ancient temples and buildings have just been left as they had fallen from an earthquake. We felt imbued with a sense of the history of the location and the importance of the ancient games and ceremonies. Blair ran the original 200-metre track in an amazing 25 seconds. It was simply magical as was our final destination at the Aldemar Olympian Village. Our hotel hosts really indulged me as I had been keen to learn all about rabbit stifado and stuffed peppers. What better place than on the beach in a top-class restaurant. Heaven.

    Finally, on our last evening we shared with our hard-working crew a magnificent feast, extra special for me as it was my birthday. And what a feast! The chef had taken Greek ingredients and themes and created something completely new: leading-edge modern Greek cuisine. Superb and a wonderful way to end our Peloponnesian adventure.

Olives marinated with lemon and fennel

Elies marinates may maratho kai lemóni

These olives were the first food we were given at Methoni and I used some of them to stuff my lamb. I couldn't wait to recreate the flavours at home. (Picture on page 84.)

Place the olives in a large bowl. Place the fennel seeds and bay leaves in a small, dry frying pan, place the pan over a medium heat and toast the seeds until fragrant. Add to the olives.

Blanch the carrot slices to soften slightly. Add the carrot, strips of lemon zest, oil and, if using, the ouzo, to the olives and stir well to combine. Cover the bowl and stand for 2 hours before serving, or refrigerate and keep for up to 1 month. Eat the marinated olives at room temperature to enjoy the flavour.

SERVES 8 as part of a meze
Preparation and cooking time
10 minutes + 2 hours standing

- 500 g large cracked, Greek green olives
- 2 tablespoons fennel seeds
- 2 bay leaves
- 1 small carrot, peeled and cut into 2 cm slices
- zest of 1 lemon, cut into very fine strips
- 1 tablespoon extra-virgin olive oil
- 1 tablespoon ouzo (optional)

Capsicums stuffed with cheese

Piperíes yemísta may tíri

This is a recipe I had tried at a Greek restaurant in Australia before we left for Greece, so I was delighted to learn how to cook it.

Preheat the oven to 200°C (180°C fan-forced). Brush a shallow baking dish with a little oil. Cut the tops off the capsicums and reserve these. Gently remove the seeds and the membrane from the capsicums, keeping them as intact as possible.

Combine the feta, graviera, oregano, parsley, basil and a little freshly ground black pepper and mix well. Squeeze handfuls of the filling together and gently push into the capsicums as far as possible — about one handful is needed to fill each. Replace the tops and place in the dish. Brush each with a little oil. Bake, uncovered, for 15–20 minutes, or until tender.

Meanwhile, to make the dressing whisk together the oil, vinegar, capers, tomatoes and rigani. Serve the hot capsicums drizzled with the dressing.

SERVES 4 as an entrée or part of a meze
Preparation and cooking time
30 minutes

4 long yellow, green or red capsicums
100 g feta, crumbled
100 g graviera or pecorino cheese, grated
1 tablespoon oregano leaves, chopped
1 tablespoon chopped flat-leaf parsley
12 basil leaves, torn
extra-virgin olive oil for brushing

Caper dressing
¼ cup extra-virgin olive oil
1 tablespoon red wine vinegar
2 teaspoons finely chopped capers
1 tablespoon finely chopped sun-dried tomatoes
¼ teaspoon rigani or dried oregano

Bandit's lamb
Kleftiko

I just had to include a recipe with a name like this, especially as it can be made with lamb or goat. While rigani is perennially evident in Greek cooking, other herbs could be used, such as dried oregano, mint or dill. The garlic is optional and thick slices of kefalograviera cheese can be placed on the lamb in place of the lemon and bay leaves.

Preheat the oven to 160°C (140°C fan-forced). Remove the seeds from the lemon slices, sprinkle the lemon slices with some kitchen salt and stand for 30 minutes. Pat dry with paper towels.

Rub the combined rigani and salt all over the lamb.

Spread out five or six sheets of baking paper on a work surface and lay the lamb in the centre. Lay the garlic slices over the top of lamb, then the lemon slices and then tuck the bay leaves among the lemon. Drizzle with the oil. Fold the paper over to enclose the lamb, tucking the sides in to ensure no cooking liquid can escape. Tie well with kitchen string to secure. Place into a roasting tin. Cook for 2¾ hours. Lift the lamb parcel onto a serving platter and cut open at the table to serve. The lamb will be meltingly tender and fall from the bone. Spoon over the juices from the parcel.

Lyndey's notes You could use a leg of lamb in place of the shoulder, if you prefer.

Don't use aluminium foil to wrap the lamb as it prevents it browning and the lamb will stew.

| SERVES 4
| Preparation and cooking time
| 3 hours + 30 minutes standing

1 lemon, finely sliced
1 tablespoon rigani
2 teaspoons sea salt flakes
1.5 kg lamb shoulder, with shank bone attached (see Lyndey's notes)
6 garlic cloves, finely sliced (optional)
5 or 6 bay leaves
2 tablespoons extra-virgin olive oil

Glorious Greek cheeses

Greeks eat cheese at any time of day, and at nearly every meal. You'll often see a simple slab of feta served as a mezedes with a glass of ouzo. Cheese is used in delicious pies like the famous Greek tiropitakia (fried cheese pies, page 209) and spanakopita (silverbeet pie, page 45). You'll see cheese sliced, grilled, baked or pan-fried, used in stuffings, in fritters, served in salads, and used to add flavour and texture in festive sweets and cakes, particularly at Easter.

Hundreds of cheeses exist in Greece, with each region or town having their own speciality. Outside Greece, feta and haloumi (actually a Cypriot cheese) are probably the best known Greek cheeses, readily available in supermarkets, and at delicatessens. Other Greek cheeses are often available in speciality cheese shops or authentic Greek produce shops. These stores are worth seeking out — their produce brings the true flavour of Greek food to your dishes.

Feta is classified as PDO (Protected Designation of Origin) and thought of as Greece's national cheese. It is used in numerous Greek recipes. Feta may have been the first preserved cheese in Greece — the Greek poet Homer mentions feta in his epic poem *The Odyssey* (believed to have been composed around the eighth century BC).

Feta can be made from sheep's or goat's milk and is matured in brine for at least two months. This crumbly, yet creamy cheese has a salty, sometimes tangy taste and can range in texture from soft to semi-hard. It is sold in slabs in brine or pre-packaged, and you can also find it sold in jars marinated with herbs and oil.

Feta's saltiness can be minimised by soaking it in cold water or milk for about 15 minutes. Slice, chop or crumble it in salads or over vegetables. Feta is not a melting cheese, yet it can be gently heated for a few minutes before serving. It can also be used to make a sauce.

Another famous cheese, haloumi, is salty and mild, sometimes enhanced with dried mint or oregano. It is quite waxy if eaten cold but is absolutely transformed when cooked. Haloumi is unique in that it can be cooked at high temperatures without melting. It is used for frying, grilling and chargrilling, when the outside will brown and become crisp while the inside softens. Remove from the brine or packaging and drain on paper towels and brush with a little oil before cooking. Some Greeks flour it first though this is not common. It is delicious served straight from the pan with a good squeeze of lemon juice.

Kefalotyri is a hard, sheep's milk and/or goat's

cheese, which is matured for three months. It has a sharp aroma and rich salty taste with a style much like Italian pecorino. It is considered to be one of Greece's best cheeses. Very versatile, it's good for grating, baking or just nibbling. Substitute pecorino or parmesan.

Kefalograviera is a very hard cheese made from sheep's milk or a blend of sheep's and goat's milk with a strong aroma and a distinctive sharp and salty flavour. Kefalotyri can be substituted.

Kasseri is a pale yellow, semi-hard cheese, often made with sheep's milk or a combination of sheep's and goat's milk, which can range in flavour from mild to sharp. It's used as a table cheese and grated in cooking as it melts easily.

Saganaki is the name of the heavy Greek frying pan used to cook the traditional cow's cheese, which is also called saganaki.

This crumbly, yet creamy cheese has a salty, sometimes tangy taste.

Saganaki can sometimes be found in Greek speciality stores; however, kefalotyri or kefalograviera are often used instead.

Manouri is a semi-soft sheep's or goat's cheese often made from the whey left over from the production of feta. It is mild, slightly sweet and very moreish. It is available from some Greek delicatessens. Alternatively use Italian-style ricotta salata.

Myzithra is a fresh cheese also made from sheep's or goat's milk whey. Fresh soft myzithra is like fresh creamy ricotta, with woven markings created by the wicker baskets it is matured in. As it is best eaten very soon after it is made, it is only really available in Greece but fresh ricotta is a good substitute. There is also a hard variety of myzithra, which is salted and aged. It is a very good grating cheese — perfect for fillings and stuffings.

Rabbit stifado

Kounéli stifádo

Stifado is a dish that has French shallots or very small onions and wine in it. The ratio is always 1 kilogram of meat to 500 grams of onions. Should you have wild rabbit, it requires longer, slow cooking. However, in Australia the most widely available rabbit is farmed and so is younger and more tender and requires less cooking.

SERVES 4
Preparation and cooking time
2 hours

Heat the oil in a large, deep frying pan (one with a lid) over a medium heat, add the red onions and cook, stirring, for 1–2 minutes to soften but not brown the onions. Add the garlic, stir for 30 seconds, then remove the onions and garlic from the pan and reserve.

Place the rabbit in the same pan, season with sea salt and freshly ground black pepper and cook until pale golden on both sides — more colour means more flavour. Return the onions and garlic to the pan with the rabbit.

Add the combined tomato paste, wine, tomatoes, stock, cinnamon, bay leaf and juniper berries. If you like, you can add extra stock or water to cover the rabbit for a thinner sauce. Reduce the heat to medium–low, cover the pan with the lid and cook for 30 minutes.

Add the shallots or pickling onions and 3 sprigs rosemary. Reduce the heat to low, cover and cook for 45 minutes (longer for wild rabbit), or until the rabbit is tender and the sauce has thickened a little.

Serve garnished with remaining rosemary sprigs.

Lyndey's note *To peel the shallots or pickling onions, cover with boiling water for 5 minutes, or until cool enough to handle. Cut off the root end and peel.*

⅓ cup extra-virgin olive oil
2 small red onions, finely chopped
2 garlic cloves, sliced
1 rabbit (about 1.25 kg), jointed
2 tablespoons tomato paste
200 ml red wine
3 tomatoes, finely chopped
400 ml light vegetable stock
1 cinnamon stick
1 bay leaf
5 whole juniper berries
600 g whole shallots or pickling onions, peeled (see Lyndey's note)
6 small rosemary sprigs

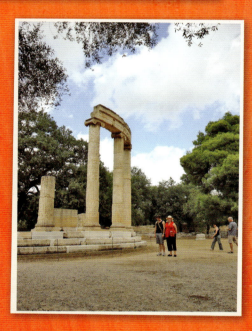

ANCIENT OLYMPIA

Everyone knows that Ancient Olympia was the site of the original Olympic Games in which only men were allowed to compete, often nude. The games were started as a way to pay homage to the god Zeus. However, not many realise that after more than a thousand years the games were stopped as they were considered pagan. What really makes the site of Olympia so amazing is the stadium, which features the original 200-metre track. It was only fully excavated after World War II.

The stadium originally seated 20,000 and the starting and finishing lines are still in place, as are the judges' thrones. Once again, Blair couldn't resist a challenge and ran the track in excellent time. Everyone was having a go, from young to old and we all entered into the spirit. With the crowd egging you on, you felt as though you could hear the roar of the crowds and imagine the athletes being crowned with wreaths of olive branches and anointed with olive oil.

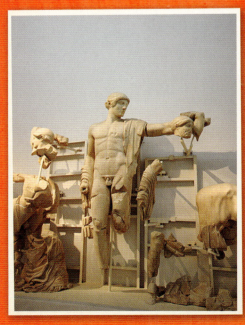

Lamb stuffed with trahanas and wine grapes

Arní yemisto may trachánas kai stafilia tou krassíou

Trahanas has been popular in Greek, Turkish and Persian cuisine for 8,000 years and is made by combining cracked wheat with fermented milk or yoghurt. This mixture is then allowed to dry before being coarsely ground. Trahanas is usually made into a thick, nourishing soup with the addition of liquid and vegetables. The sweet version is typically eaten for breakfast, but here it counteracts the acidity of the wine. You can find trahanas at speciality Mediterranean and Middle Eastern delicatessens. Burghul, couscous, quinoa or even rice are good substitutes.

SERVES 6
Preparation and cooking time
2 hours + 15 minutes resting

To make the stuffing, heat half the oil in a medium frying pan, add the onion and garlic and cook over a medium heat for 5 minutes, or until softened. Add the trahanas and stir until coated with oil. Add the water and cook, stirring frequently as it begins to thicken. Then add 1 cup of the wine and cook until the grains are just tender and the mixture is thick. Remove from the heat and cool. When cool, add the walnuts, grapes, olives and rigani and season to taste with salt and freshly ground black pepper and mix well.

Place the lamb, fat side down, on the workbench and spoon over the stuffing. Fold the meat over to cover the stuffing and, tucking in all edges, tie the lamb securely with kitchen string, ensuring that the stuffing is fully encased. If available, grape leaves or foil can be placed over the ends to prevent any stuffing escaping during cooking.

Heat the remaining oil in a large, heavy saucepan over a high heat. Add the lamb and cook, turning frequently until golden on all sides. Pour over the remaining wine, reduce the heat, cover with the lid and cook for 1 hour 45 minutes, or until the lamb is very tender, making sure to check the liquid every 20 minutes and topping up with more wine or water if required. Alternatively, cook in the oven (see Lyndey's note).

Remove from the heat and allow the lamb to rest for at least 15 minutes. Remove the string, slice the lamb and serve drizzled with the pan juices and crusty bread.

Lyndey's note *After browning, the lamb can be cooked in a preheated (180°C/160°C fan-forced) oven; cook for the same length of time, basting every 30 minutes.*

1.75 kg leg or shoulder of lamb, boned

Trahanas and grape stuffing
½ cup extra-virgin olive oil
1 red onion, finely chopped
3 garlic cloves, finely chopped
¾ cup sweet trahanas (see recipe introduction)
1 cup water
3 cups white wine
½ cup walnuts, chopped
135 g wine or table grapes, cut into halves and deseeded
½ cup olives, pitted and cut into halves
2 tablespoons rigani or dried oregano

Swordfish souvlaki with capers and dill

Souvláki ksiféas may capári kai aníthos

While souvlaki is traditionally made with pork, seafood makes a lovely change. Swordfish has a firm texture that holds together well on the skewers.

Thread the swordfish onto eight skewers, beginning and ending each skewer with a bay leaf. Alternate a cube of fish with a bay leaf, if you like.

Combine the capers, dill, lemon zest and juice, oil and salt. Take one-third of the mixture and brush it over the swordfish. Reserve the remaining mixture to serve with the fish.

Preheat a chargrill pan to medium–high, brush the pan with a little oil, add the skewers and cook for 2–3 minutes on each side, or until just cooked through. Turn once only.

Serve the swordfish skewers with the remaining caper and dill mixture.

Lyndey's note *If using wooden skewers, soak in water for 20 minutes or freeze overnight; this stops them burning.*

SERVES 4
Preparation and cooking time
20 minutes

700 g swordfish steaks, skin removed, cut into 3 cm cubes
16 small fresh bay leaves
⅓ cup capers, chopped
½ bunch dill, chopped
grated zest and juice 1 large lemon
⅓ cup extra-virgin olive oil
1 teaspoon sea salt flakes

Chicken stuffed with artichokes, fennel and sundried tomatoes

Kotópolo yemisto may angináres maratho kai liastres tomátes

This was one of the modern dishes served to us for our final dinner at the Aldemar.

Preheat the oven to 180°C (160°C fan-forced). Heat a medium frying pan over a medium heat and add half of the oil. Add the fennel, artichokes, sundried tomatoes and half of the green onions and 1 garlic clove. Cook, stirring, for 1–2 minutes to soften the fennel. Add half of the wine and let it evaporate. Remove the pan from the heat and transfer the fennel mixture to a bowl. Allow the mixture to cool slightly, then stir in the graviera, thyme and oregano. Season well with salt and freshly ground black pepper.

Place the fennel mixture under skin of the chicken fillets, then roll each chicken fillet to form a cylinder; tie with kitchen string to secure. Heat a medium frying pan over a medium heat, add half of the remaining oil and cook the chicken fillets on all sides until golden. Transfer to the oven and cook for 15–20 minutes, or until the chicken is cooked through.

In a small saucepan, add the remaining oil, remaining green onion and remaining garlic clove and cook, stirring, until soft, then add the remaining wine along with the stock and sage. Bring to the boil, reduce the heat and simmer until reduced by half.

Place another pan over a medium heat. Add a splash of oil and gently wilt the baby spinach along with the tomatoes. Place on a serving dish.

Remove the chicken from the oven, remove the string, place the chicken on top of the spinach and tomatoes and drizzle with the sauce.

SERVES 4
Preparation and cooking time 50 minutes

- ⅓ cup extra-virgin olive oil
- 1 small fennel bulb, finely sliced
- 8 (about 100 g) marinated artichoke hearts, drained
- ½ cup sundried tomatoes, finely chopped
- 2 green onions (shallots), finely chopped
- 2 garlic cloves, finely chopped
- ¼ cup white wine
- ½ cup grated graviera or parmesan cheese
- ¼ cup mixed fresh thyme and oregano leaves, finely chopped
- 4 (about 200 g each) single chicken breast fillets, skin on, pounded slightly to flatten
- 2 cups veal or chicken stock
- 1 tablespoon chopped fresh sage
- 125 g baby spinach leaves
- 125 g cherry tomatoes

Snapper with walnut crust and citrus–pomegranate syrup

Sinagrída may cróusta karídia kai lemóni ródi sirópi

This is my version of another of the lovely dishes we enjoyed for our finale at the Aldemar restaurant.

SERVES 4
Preparation and cooking time
25 minutes

To make the syrup, place the orange juice, grapefruit juice, pomegranate juice and sugar in a small saucepan, bring to the boil, then reduce the heat and simmer until the mixture is reduced to about ¾ cup and is syrupy.

Meanwhile, to make the crust, process the walnuts and bread into crumbs with a food processor or blender. Add the graviera and butter and season with salt and freshly ground black pepper. Pulse for a further 30 seconds — do not allow it to turn to paste. Make sure the crust is well seasoned.

To cook the fish, preheat an oven grill to hot. Heat a large ovenproof frying pan over a medium–high heat, add the oil, heat, then add the snapper fillets, skin side down. Cook for 1 minute, then turn and cook for a further 2 minutes.

Top the fillets evenly with the crust. Place the pan under the preheated grill for 3 minutes, or until the fillets are just cooked and the crust is golden.

Serve the fish with the rocket leaves. Drizzle with the citrus–pomegranate syrup.

Lyndey's note To make fresh pomegranate juice, cut the pomegranate in half. Place the halves in a large bowl of water for a few minutes, and then pull the pieces apart as you hold them under the water. Working under the water, use a small spoon to scoop the arils from the white pith. Discard the zest and pith, and then drain. Dry the arils on paper towels. Then blend or process to get the juice, strain before using. Pomegranate juice stains, so take care.

Rather than using fresh pomegranate juice, you can substitute it in the sauce with grapefruit or orange juice, and add pomegranate molasses to taste. As pomegranate molasses is a concentrated syrup, you shouldn't need to use much.

2 tablespoons extra-virgin olive oil
4 small or 8 medium snapper fillets (or other firm-fleshed fish fillets)
rocket leaves (arugula) to serve

Walnut crust
½ cup chopped walnuts
1 slice good-quality white sourdough bread
¼ cup grated graviera cheese or pecorino
30 g cold butter, cut into small cubes

Citrus–pomegranate syrup
1 cup fresh orange juice (about 3 oranges)
⅔ cup fresh grapefruit juice (1 large grapefruit)
200 ml fresh pomegranate juice (juice of 2 pomegranates) (see Lyndey's note)
⅓ cup sugar

Braised veal with eggplant purée

Moschári sti kaseróla may melitzána puráys

I've used bay leaves a lot in this chapter as successful athletes at Olympia were crowned with a laurel or bay wreath. This is the most satisfying dish, the luscious veal enriched with the silky eggplant purée.

SERVES 4
Preparation and cooking time 1¾ hours

Preheat the oven to 180°C (160°C fan-forced). Drizzle half of the oil over the veal cubes, mix well and season the veal with a little salt and freshly ground black pepper.

Heat a large flameproof casserole dish (one with a lid), over a medium–high heat. Brown the veal in three batches, reheating the dish between batches.

Add the remaining oil to the dish, add the onions and cook, stirring, for 1 minute to soften but not brown the onions. Add the wine, stock, cloves, juniper berries and bay leaves and let the mixture come to the boil. Return all of the veal to the dish, stirring to mix. Cover with the lid and place in the oven. Cook, stirring the veal once or twice, for 1 hour.

Meanwhile, to make the purée, prick the eggplants all over with a fork. Place the eggplants directly on an oven rack, with a tray underneath the rack. Roast for 30–40 minutes, or until the eggplants are soft, turning them once or twice. Remove from the oven and stand the eggplants in a colander to drain the juices for 10 minutes. When cool enough to handle, cut the eggplants in half, spoon the flesh into a food processor and process until smooth.

When the veal has cooked for about 1 hour, stir in the tomato purée, cover and cook for a further 30 minutes, or until the veal is tender. Remove the cloves, juniper and bay leaves, if you like. Stand for 5 minutes while you heat the eggplant.

Heat the eggplant purée in small frying pan and whisk in the butter a little at a time; once the butter has been incorporated, whisk in the milk.

To serve, place a spoonful of the eggplant purée onto a warm dinner plate or shallow bowl, add a ladleful of braised veal and sprinkle with parsley leaves.

⅓ cup extra-virgin olive oil
1.2 kg leg or shoulder of veal, cut into 3 cm cubes
2 red onions, chopped
1 cup red wine
1½ cups beef stock
4 cloves
3–4 whole juniper berries
2 bay leaves
1 cup tomato purée
flat-leaf parsley to serve

Eggplant purée
2 (1 kg) large eggplants (aubergines)
125 g butter
¼ cup milk

Rabbit with rosemary and garlic in white wine

Kounéli krassáto may dentrolívano kai skórdo

Now that farmed rabbit is available it is much quicker and simpler to cook. Here it has the tastes of Greece: white wine, garlic, fresh herbs and lemon. It is absolutely delicious with the trahanas stuffing (served as a side) from the recipe for lamb stuffed with trahanas and wine grapes (page 197).

Heat the oil in a large, deep frying pan (one with a lid) over a medium heat. Season the rabbit with salt and freshly ground black pepper and cook until pale golden on both sides — more colour means more flavour.

Return all the rabbit pieces to the pan and then add the garlic. When the garlic is lightly browned, add the wine, bay leaf, rosemary and water.

Cover with the lid, reduce the heat to low and simmer for 40–45 minutes, or until the rabbit is tender. Add the lemon juice, shaking the dish gently to mix in. Turn off the heat and leave to stand for 10 minutes before serving.

Lyndey's note *This dish can also be prepared the day before and gently reheated before serving.*

SERVES 4
Preparation and cooking time
55 minutes + 10 minutes standing

¼ cup extra-virgin olive oil
1 rabbit (about 1.25 kg), jointed
12 garlic cloves, cut in slivers lengthwise
½ cup white wine
1 bay leaf
2 rosemary sprigs
2 cups water
juice of 2 lemons

Ouzo frappé

Ouzo frappé

Ouzo jelly was the starting point for this idea, as was the ubiquitous 'Greek frappé' drunk everywhere in Greece. Use glasses to get the full visual effect of a Greek frappé.

To make the jelly, combine the water and sugar in a medium saucepan and stir over a medium heat for 5–6 minutes, or until the mixture comes to a simmer. Simmer for 5 minutes. Remove from the heat and stir in the coffee powder and ouzo. Soak the gelatine sheets in ice-cold water for 5 minutes, then squeeze out the excess water. Add the gelatine to the coffee mixture, and whisk to thoroughly combine.

Place six 1-cup glasses on a tray. Divide the jelly among the glasses. Refrigerate for 1–2 hours to set the jelly.

Once the jelly is set, make the frappé. Heat the cream, sugar and chocolate in a small saucepan over a low heat and stir until the sugar and chocolate have completely melted. Remove from the heat, then cool the mixture. Soak the gelatine sheet in ice-cold water for 5 minutes, squeeze out the excess water, add the gelatine to the chocolate mixture along with the vanilla and ouzo, and whisk to thoroughly combine.

Gently pour the white chocolate mixture over the coffee jelly. Refrigerate for 2–3 hours to set.

Lyndey's note You can replace the Greek coffee powder with 60 ml strong espresso, if you like.

SERVES 6
Preparation and cooking time
20 minutes + 3–5 hours setting or overnight

Coffee–ouzo jelly
1½ cups water
½ cup sugar
2 tablespoons Greek coffee powder (see Lyndey's note)
⅓ cup ouzo
2 sheets (5 g each sheet) leaf gelatine

White chocolate–ouzo frappé
2 cups cream
⅓ cup caster sugar
180 g white chocolate, broken into pieces
1 sheet (5 g) leaf gelatine
¼ teaspoon vanilla essence
2 tablespoons ouzo

GREEK SWEETS

I've never met a Greek who doesn't have a sweet tooth. Sweets are eaten usually as a separate course, either in the morning or early evening. Greeks eat their main course in the middle of the day so late afternoon when the heat is subsiding they go out for 'coffee'. Wherever you go you see large trays of sticky, tiny baklava with pistachios or walnuts pressed into them, bowls of spoon sweets, from fig to quince in a myriad of colours, and baskets of cookies. All of them are served with a glass of ice-cold water or a bitter cup of Greek coffee. The evening promenade sees families eating ices and sipping sweet iced coffee or spooning a sweet slice of custard tart into their mouths. Every area has its own specialities and everyone their own grandmother's recipe, which of course is the best they've ever tasted!

Fried cheese pies
Tirópitákia

I first made these after a trip to Greece in 2006 when I became fascinated with olive oil pastry. I created these little pies for *Fresh with The Australian Women's Weekly* on the Nine Network where I was co-host for eight years. They are worth sharing again.

To make the pastry, combine the flour, salt, oil, egg and water in a large bowl or food processor and work together either by hand or with the food processor. Cover and rest in the refrigerator for 30 minutes.

To make the filling, combine the feta, myzithra cheese, kefalograviera cheese, mint and eggs.

Roll the dough out to a thin sheet and cut into rounds about 8 cm across. Place 2 teaspoons of the filling in the middle of each round. Brush the edges with water and fold over to form a semicircle, squeeze together using the tines of a fork.

To cook the pastries, heat the oil in a large frying pan over a medium heat. Test the heat of the oil with a wooden implement to see if bubbles appear. Fry the pastries, three or four at a time, for 1–2 minutes on each side, or until golden and cooked through. Drain on paper towels. Serve immediately.

MAKES 24
Preparation and cooking time
30 minutes + 30 minutes standing

Olive oil pastry
3⅓ cups plain flour
1 teaspoon salt
⅓ cup extra-virgin olive oil
1 egg, lightly beaten
¾ cup cold water

Cheese filling
2 cups grated feta
1 cup grated, unsalted myzithra cheese or ricotta salata
1 cup grated kefalograviera or pecorino cheese
½ teaspoon dried mint
2 eggs, lightly beaten

1 cup extra-virgin olive oil for frying

GLOSSARY

GREEK COOKING METHODS

The cooking methods used in Greece are usually fairly simple and straightforward. Many recipes and accompanying methods have been handed down through the generations, with little adaptation. Further, often the name of the dish reflects the method of preparation and/or the cooking vessel. Although Greece has diverse geography and climate, many cooking methods are universal across different regions, such as the following.

Avgolemono is the light egg and lemon sauce known to adorn spring artichokes and peas as well as to add flavour to pork fricassee and fish soup.

Kokkinisto means red and this is always a tomato-based baked dish, usually with beef or chicken.

Ladi is Greek olive oil and **ladera** refers to dishes prepared with lots of olive oil.

The best example of **o graten,** meaning a dish covered with béchamel sauce and cheese, is the most famous Greek dish of all, moussaka.

Plaki, meaning flat or spread out, usually refers to fish arranged flat in a baking dish and baked in the oven.

Psito means roasted and this is how the Greeks like their pork, wild boar and lamb.

Saganaki refers to the skillet or heavy cast-iron frying pan used in the cooking process. A very popular meze dish of Greek cheese, such as kefalotyri or kefalograviera, dusted with flour and fried in olive oil in this style of vessel is also referred to as saganaki.

Stifado indicates the addition of tiny pearl onions and cinnamon to a dish.

Stis skara or **tis oras** means at the hour and denotes food that is cooked on the charcoal grill at the last minute.

Sto fourno literally means 'in the oven'. Any dishes cooked in a claypot are all prepared using this method.

Tiganita refers to food that is shallow-fried in olive oil.

Vrasto means boiled and usually applies to wild greens picked during the rainy season.

Yachni is a hearty tomato-based stew often served with tiny pasta shapes.

GREEK DRY INGREDIENTS

Like all cuisines, the ingredients used in Greek cookery tend to be sourced locally and often their availability is dependent on seasonality.

The spice **anise**, used to make **ouzo**, adds a lovely flavour to many breads and pastries.

Capers are picked in spring and preserved in a vinegar solution or salt. The dark green buds are often used to enhance the flavour of salads.

Greece is famous for its **cheeses** and at least one type of cheese is usually served at each mealtime. See pages 192–93 for more about Greek cheese.

Cinnamon is a very popular spice and features in both savoury dishes, such as moussaka, and sweet, such as sticky baklava.

Dried fakes (small green-brown lentils) are used in a soup during the winter with a little onion and dill. **Fava** (**split yellow peas**) are used for a dip with oil and onion (page 75). **Chickpeas** are used to make hummus or for chickpea fritters and in salads.

Filo is the paper-thin unleavened flour-based pastry that is used widely in Greek cooking. Uses include the famous spanakopita, spinach and feta pie to sticky nut-filled baklava drenched with honey syrup.

Grape must syrup (in Greek, pronounced MOOstohs) or **petimezi** is a by-product of the grape. It is the sweet grape juice that is cooked down until it forms sweet syrup and used to flavour desserts and biscuits. It can be light or dark depending on the type of grape used.

Like olives, the **grapes** of Greece are hugely significant, not only for the wine they produce, but also the vinegar, grape must and verjuice, vine leaves and dried grapes they provide. Plump **raisins**, sweet golden **sultanas** from Corinth and tiny **currants** find their way into many Greek dishes.

Mahlab is the soft nut-like kernel inside cherry seeds and imparts a strong cherry flavour in baking, particularly in pastries and Easter breads.

The forerunner of chewing gum, **mastica** is a gum that comes only from the mastic trees which grow on the island of Chios, the fifth largest of the Greek Islands. An aromatic gum resin, it is chewed to sweeten the breath. Dried and powdered, it is used to flavour ice cream, biscuits, cakes and breads.

Olive oil, especially extra-virgin, the quintessential Greek seasoning, is universally popular and olives are harvested and eaten all over Greece. Generally the idea is that this year's oil (from olives harvested from November until February) is used for salads and dressing vegetables or dishes once cooked. All other oil, including the previous year's oil is used for frying and adding to cooked ladera dishes.

Paximadia are lightly sweetened twice-baked barley rusks available from bakeries. As well as being enjoyed dipped in coffee, they are also moistened with water and served topped with tomato and cheese, or in a salad or eaten with cheese for breakfast.

Grilled or roasted **pork** is probably the most important meat, closely followed by lamb, which is especially popular during the Easter period.

Greek Orthodox faithful traditionally fast for 40 days before Easter and Christmas (and many other days throughout the year). During this time meat and dairy products are excluded from their diet. **Pulses** such as **chickpeas**, **lentils** and other **dried beans** form the basis of various dishes during this fasting time.

Rigani, dried Greek oregano, is the most important herb in Greek cuisine. It is worth sourcing from Greek and European specialist food shops as it adds a very authentic flavour. Wonderfully aromatic, rigani is put on top of feta in Greek salad, even on chips (but not put into pitas with spinach or cheese). Teamed with lamb, goat, chicken and vegetables it is found in many recipes.

Verjuice, the unfermented juice of unripe grapes is also made and used in place of lemon juice when lemons are unavailable.

Wine vinegar is called for in many Greek recipes, notably the red wine and garlic seasoning skordóstoumbi (page 22). White, red and flavoured barrel-aged vinegars are produced. Fig-sweetened aged vinegar is a speciality from Kalamata. Greek vinegars are generally low in acetic acid, making them not as sharp as some others — perfect for dressing salads.

Thick Greek **yoghurt** made from cow's or sheep's milk is used in dips and as an accompaniment to fruit-based desserts. It is also a popular breakfast with tourists, especially drizzled with local Greek honey and sprinkled with walnuts. It can equally be enjoyed as a dessert.

GREEK FRESH INGREDIENTS

Vegetables are plentiful in the Greek diet and take centrestage on Greek plates. They can be part of a meal served in the middle of the table, or even a main course, prepared in myriad ways: baked, fried, braised, stuffed, grilled and used plentifully in salads, stews, soups and casseroles.

Greeks eat seasonally, cooking what is fresh and available. The braised vegetable dishes that feature on spring and summer menus throughout the Peloponnese are a good example of the Greek cook's approach to seasonality. They are likely to feature just one or two in-season vegetables, which will be simply prepared, most often cooked with onions and/or garlic, tomatoes and steeped liberally in local extra-virgin olive oil.

Fresh ingredients tend to be sourced locally so their availability is dependent on seasonality. The following are some of the most important vegetables and other fresh ingredients used in Greek cuisine or important to their culture.

Basil is prolific during the summer — it grows everywhere — and although used in religious ceremonies it is rarely used in cooking.

Fresh **dill** is very popular, so much so that whole bunches are often used in dishes.

Eggplant (**aubergine**) is the central ingredient in Greece's most famous dish, moussaka. However, eggplants are also used in salad, fried in fritters, stuffed for delicious dishes like imam bayaldi or papoutsakia (page 113) and used in lamb and goat casseroles. The long, thin eggplants grown in the town of Leonidio in the Peloponnese even have their own festival when chefs from across Europe come to judge the best eggplant dishes.

Sweet perfumed **figs** are eaten fresh during their summer season, or dried in the sun to be enjoyed year-round in many sweet dishes.

Flat-leaf parsley is used extensively in Greek cooking.

Liberal amounts of **garlic** are added to many savoury dishes (*see also* Onions and garlic, page 215).

Globe artichokes are a springtime staple, particularly in the Peloponnese. They're cooked in a many ways, with braised artichokes (page 92) being the most popular.

Grapevines grow over the walls and pergolas in many Greek homes. Families will often preserve their own fresh, young and tender vine leaves in a brine solution or by freezing. The dried fruit — plump raisins, sweet golden sultanas from Corinth and tiny currants — finds its way into many Greek dishes.

Greeks love their greens, and enjoy them regularly. **Horta** literally means greens and in Greece everyone eats the wild greens that appear in the fields after the first autumn rains, with over 30 varieties collected locally. Boiled and dressed with lemon and oil, they are said to be very good for you. They also eat farmed summer horta called **vlita** in Greek, which is often sold in Asian supermarkets under the name **amaranth** or **Chinese greens** (**en choy**) and are easy to spot as they have a deep red flush on the leaf. Long green-leafed chicory works well too.

Lemons are ever-present in Greek cooking. They are squeezed over nearly everything, particularly fried food.

Dried and fresh **mint** is a favourite herb, used in many savoury dishes, particularly those featuring tomatoes or cheese. It is added to filo pastry pie fillings, especially those containing greens such as spinach and selino.

Onions and **garlic** are ever present in Greek cooking — it's not a Greek dish without one or the other (or both)! Liberal amounts of garlic are added to many savoury dishes. **Red onions** with their sweet flavour are used in just about everything, fried in plenty of oil. Onions are also sometimes cooked until very soft, stirred until they form almost an emulsion and served with goat and oil, or chicken and feta. **Green onions** (**shallots**) are used often too, especially in lettuce salad and in the famous filo and silverbeet pie, spanakopita (page 45).

Fresh or dried **oregano** (*see also* rigani, page 213) is sprinkled on cheese dishes, such as the famous Greek salad with feta (see village salad, page 60) as well as fried potatoes.

Potatoes are widely eaten all over Greece. They are used in most baked dishes featuring chicken, and are often roasted with lamb and pork. They are often finished with lemon juice as well as layered with other vegetables and cooked 'plaki' style. Potatoes are also integral to the Greek sauce, skordalia.

Selino or **wild celery**, is both a herb and a vegetable. With thinner stalks and more leaves than regular celery, is often used with onion and carrot as the base of many stews and soups. A combination of celery stalks and flat-leaf parsley can be substituted.

Spinach, or more commonly **silverbeet**, is used in the famous pie, spanakopita (page 45), but is also mixed with black-eyed beans or rice for a light meal.

Fresh peas, **fresh broad beans** and **green beans** are important vegetables. Often paired with lemon or tomato, they form the basis of many spring dishes.

Thyme is used in the same way as oregano, though it is sprinkled on as opposed to used in dishes.

Picked in late spring, **vine leaves** are first blanched in boiling water to soften and then preserved for up to one year in brine. Their most common use is to wrap dolmades (see meat-stuffed dolmades, page 88).

Zucchini (courgette) figures prominently in summer cooking, in meze dishes, salads and meat dishes. Zucchini in Greece are sliced and fried in oil or sliced and dipped in batter for fritters, or often stuffed with mince. Zucchini flowers are filled with cheese, usually feta, or with rice and herbs and then fried (see ouzo-battered zucchini flowers stuffed with goat's curd, page 110).

USEFUL INFORMATION

CUP CONVERSIONS FOR SOME COMMON DRY INGREDIENTS

Almonds, ground 1 cup = 120 g
Breadcrumbs, fresh 1 cup = 70 g
Cheese, grated kefalotyri or kefalograviera
  1 cup = 120 g
Cheese, grated pecorino 1 cup = 80 g
Flour ¼ cup = 35 g
Flour ⅓ cup = 50 g
Flour ½ cup = 75 g
Flour 1 cup = 150 g
Flour 1¼ cups = 185 g
Flour 1⅓ cups = 200 g
Flour 1½ cups = 225 g
Rice 1 cup = 200 g
Risoni (rice-shaped pasta) 1 cup = 220 g
Semolina 1 cup = 160 g
Sugar, caster 1 cup = 220 g
Sugar, firmly packed soft brown 1 cup = 220 g
Sugar, icing 1 cup = 160 g
Sugar, white 1 cup = 220 g

LIQUID MEASURES

1 cup = 250 ml
¾ cup = 180 ml
⅔ cup = 160 ml
½ cup = 125 ml
⅓ cup = 80 ml
¼ cup = 60 ml
1 Australian metric tablespoon = 20 ml
1 Australian teaspoon = 5 ml

* All cup and spoon measures are level.
* Eggs with an average weight of 60 g were used for all recipes.

BIBLIOGRAPHY

Alexiadou, Vefa, *Vefa's Kichen*, Phaidon Press Ltd, London, 2009.
Culinaria Greek: Greece Specialities, Konemann, Tandem Verlag, 2004.
Greek Gourmet Traveller, Nos 4—13, Hellenic Foreign Trade Board.
Kyritsis, Janni, *Wild Weed Pie*, Penguin, Australia, 2006.
Psilakis, Michael, *How to Roast a Lamb: New Greek Classic Cooking*, Little Brown and Company, New York, 2009.
Souli, Sophia, *Greek Cookery and Wines*, Michael Toubis Publications, Attiki, 1997.

Page numbers in *italics* refer to photographs

A
Acrocorinth 58, *58*
Aldemar Olympian Village 187
almonds
    goat's curd with strawberries and toasted almonds 120, *121*
    Greek shortbread cookies *176*, 177
    Kythirian koumara 119
    rozedes 118
    sesame bars 125
amaranth 48, 214
anchovies, marinated 131
anise 212
artichoke hearts
    fennel, artichoke and broad bean salad *64*, 65
    fried calamari and artichokes 56, *57*
    see also globe artichokes
Athens *16*, 19
aubergine see eggplant
avgolemono 212

B
baklava 208
bandit's lamb *190*, 191
barbounia wrapped in vine leaves 46, *47*
basil 214
beef
    meat-stuffed dolmades 88
    stuffed eggplants *112*, 113
beetroot, feta and walnuts, salad of *98*, 99
black-eyed peas and herbs, slow-roasted lamb with salad of 144, *145*
blood of Hercules 25, *27*
Bourtzi *78*, 78
briam of potato and zucchini 93
broad beans 215
    artichokes with broad beans and lemon *132*, 133
    fennel, artichoke and broad bean salad *64*, 65

C
cabbage slaw 87
calamari see squid
calvolo nero
    wild greens pie 116, *117*
Cape Tenaro *152*, 152
capers 212
    caper dressing 189
    swordfish souvlaki with capers and dill *198*, 199
capsicum
    braised artichokes 92
    capsicums stuffed with cheese 189
    prawns and scallops in kataifi with spicy capsicum skordalia *158*, 159
    spetzofai 89
    village salad 60, *63*
cauliflower salad 61, *62*
celery
    lamb fricassee *166*, 167
    lentil and chickpea salad 149

cheese 192–3, 212
    see also feta; goat's cheese/curd; haloumi; kefalotyri; manouri; pecorino; ricotta; saganaki
cheesecake with muscatels 36, *37*
cherry tomatoes 200
chicken
    chicken stuffed with artichokes, fennel and sundried tomatoes 200
    cockerel or chicken in wine with potatoes 169
    Peloponnesian-style roast chicken 142
chickpeas 212, 213
    chickpea fritters with a salad of rocket and raisins 35
    lentil and chickpea salad 149
chicory 116, *117*
chillies
    prawns and scallops in kataifi with spicy capsicum skordalia *158*, 159
    spetzofai 89
Chinese greens 215
chocolate
    Kythirian koumara 119
    ouzo frappé 206, *207*
cinnamon 212
citron vodka 24
cockerel or chicken in wine with potatoes 169
cocktails
    blood of Hercules 25, *27*
    ginger and lime daiquiri 24, *26*
    long sparkling ouzo 25, *27*
    red rock 24, *27*
    sparkling watermelon with ouzo foam 25, *26*
    under the Hellenic sun 24, *26*
cod fritters with tzatziki, salt *85*, 115
coffee 179, *179*
coffee-ouzo jelly 206, *207*
Cointreau 24
cooking methods, Greek 212
Corinth Canal *38*, 38
corn, pumpkin, goat's cheese and saffron, risotto with charred *32*, 33
courgettes see zucchini
cream cheese
    cheesecake with muscatels 36, *37*
cucumber
    village salad 60, *63*
    yoghurt garlic dip 74, *76*
currants 213

D
daiquiri, ginger and lime 24, *26*
dill 214
    swordfish souvlaki with capers and dill *198*, 199
    zucchini, dill and mint fritters 80, *81*
diples 150, *151*
dips
    feta 75, *76*
    split pea 75, *77*
    yoghurt garlic 74, *76*
Diros caves 134, *134*

dolmades, meat-stuffed 88
dried beans 213
dry ingredients 212–13

E
Easter 172–3, *174–5*, 192
Easter bread 173, *175*
eggplant 214
    braised eggplant and fresh fennel with tomato and fennel seed 135
    braised goat with eggplant 53
    braised veal with eggplant purée 202, *203*
    eggplant salad *106*, 107
    eggplant sauce 34
    stuffed eggplants *112*, 113
eggs
    cheese sauce 23
    cheesecake with muscatels 36, *37*
    fried cheese pies 209
    Greek creamed rice 153
    red eggs 172, 173, *174*
    silverbeet pie *44*, 45
    walnut, orange and olive oil cake with spice syrup 178
en choy 215
Epidavros 52, *52*

F
fakes, dried 212
fava 212
fennel
    braised eggplant and fresh fennel with tomato and fennel seed 135
    chicken stuffed with artichokes, fennel and sundried tomatoes 200
    fennel, artichoke and broad bean salad *64*, 65
    haloumi with fennel, orange and kalamata olives 161
    Mediterranean fish soup 139
fennel seed 135
    braised eggplant and fresh fennel with tomato and fennel seed 135
    chargrilled manouri served with honey-baked peaches *122*, 123
    eggplant salad *106*, 107
    olives marinated with lemon and fennel *84*, 188
    slow-roasted lamb with salad of black-eyed peas and herbs 144, *145*
feta, 82, 192
    barbecued squid filled with spinach and feta *50*, 51
    braised veal with orzo *94*, 95
    country-style macaroni pie 59
    feta dip 75, *76*
    fried cheese pies 209
    salad of beetroot, feta and walnuts *98*, 99
    salad of black-eyed peas and herbs 144, *145*
    silverbeet pie *44*, 45, 192
    slow-roasted lamb ribs with yoghurt and feta sauce 90, *91*

village salad 60, *63*
wild greens pie 116, *117*
figs 214
    filo rolls with manouri, walnuts, raisins, figs and mint 180, *181*
    Greek yoghurt and honey ice cream with a warm syrupy dried fig spoon sweet 39
filo 213
    filo rolls with manouri, walnuts, raisins, figs and mint 180, *181*
fish *see* seafood
flat-leaf parsley 214
flying squid in garlic and olive oil 67
fresh ingredients 214–15
fritters
    chickpea with a salad of rocket and raisins 35
    salt cod with tzatziki *85*, 115
    zucchini, dill and mint 80, *81*

G
garlic 214, 215
    flying squid in garlic and olive oil 67
    garlic marinade 162
    garlic walnut crumb 143
    rabbit with rosemary and garlic in white wine *204*, 205
    yoghurt garlic dip 74, *76*
gigantes braised with tomato 109
ginger and lime daiquiri 24, *26*
globe artichokes *92*, 214
    artichokes with broad beans and lemon *132*, 133
    braised artichokes 92
    chicken stuffed with artichokes, fennel and sundried tomatoes 200
    see also artichoke hearts
goat with eggplant, braised 53
goat's cheese/curd 192, 193
    chargrilled manouri served with honey-baked peaches *122*, 123
    cheesecake with muscatels 36, *37*
    goat's curd with strawberries and toasted almonds 120, *121*
    ouzo-battered zucchini flowers stuffed with goat's curd 110, *111*
    risotto with charred corn, pumpkin, goat's cheese and saffron *32*, 33
grape must syrup 213
grapefruit juice
    snapper with walnut crust and citrus-pomegranate syrup 201
grapes, lamb stuffed with trahanas and wine grapes 197
graviera
    capsicums stuffed with cheese 189
    chicken stuffed with artichokes, fennel and sundried tomatoes 200
    snapper with walnut crust and citrus-pomegranate syrup 201
Greek coffee 179, *179*
Greek creamed rice 153
Greek 'fish fingers' with lemon mayonnaise 97
Greek shortbread cookies *176*, 177

Greek-style yoghurt 213
    feta dip 75, *76*
    Greek yoghurt and honey, 68, *69*
    Greek yoghurt and honey ice cream with a warm syrupy dried fig spoon sweet 39
    lamb fricassee *166*, 167
    slow-roasted lamb ribs with yoghurt and feta sauce 90, *91*
    walnut, orange and olive oil cake with spice syrup 178
    yoghurt garlic dip 74, *76*
Greek sweets 208, *208*
green beans 215
green beans and potato, braised *146*, 147
green onions 215
    chicken stuffed with artichokes, fennel and sundried tomatoes 200
    feta and green onion stuffing 51
    fried pumpkin balls 130
    lamb fricassee *166*, 167
    rabbit stifado 194, *195*
    salt cod fritters with tzatziki *85*, 115
    silverbeet pie 44, 45
    silverbeet pilaf 148
    wild greens pie 116, *117*

H–I
Hades 152, *152*
haloumi 192
    country-style macaroni pie 59
    haloumi with fennel, orange and kalamata olives 161
honey, 183, *183*
    baby octopus marinated in honey 31, *84*
    chargrilled manouri served with honey-baked peaches *122*, 123
    diples 150, *151*
    Greek yoghurt and honey 68, *69*
    Greek yoghurt and honey ice cream with a warm syrupy dried fig spoon sweet 39
    Kythirian koumara 119
    loukoumades with honey syrup 182
    rozedes 118
    sesame bars 125
horta 214
ice cream with a warm syrupy dried fig spoon sweet, Greek yoghurt and honey 39

K
Kalamata 157
Kalogria 138, *138*
kasseri 65, 193
kataifi with spicy capsicum skordalia prawns and scallops in *158*, 159
kefalograviera 193
    fried cheese pies 209
kefalotyri 193
    braised veal with orzo *94*, 95
    fennel, artichoke and broad bean salad *64*, 65
    ouzo-battered zucchini flowers stuffed with goat's curd 110, *111*

pastitsio 23
stuffed eggplants *112*, 113
zucchini, dill and mint fritters 80, *81*
keftedes, 82
    braised pork keftedes flavoured with ouzo 28, *29*
    lamb keftedes 34, *85*
kokkinisto 212
koumara, Kythirian 119
Kythira 105, 124, *124*
Kythirian koumara 119

L
ladera 212
ladi 212
lamb
    bandit's lamb *190*, 191
    lamb fricassee *166*, 167
    lamb keftedes 34, *85*
    lamb stuffed with trahanas and wine grapes 197
    pastitsio 23
    slow-roasted lamb ribs with yoghurt and feta sauce 90, *91*
    slow-roasted lamb with salad of black-eyed peas and herbs 144, *145*
leek stuffing 49
lemons 214
    artichokes with broad beans and lemon *132*, 133
    bandit's lamb *190*, 191
    lemon mayonnaise 97
    olives marinated with lemon and fennel *84*, 188
    rabbit with rosemary and garlic in white wine *204*, 205
    roast pork with lemon potatoes *140*, 141
    swordfish souvlaki with capers and dill *198*, 199
lentil and chickpea salad 149
lentils 213
lettuce
    lamb fricassee *166*, 167
    marouli salad 60, *62*
lima beans
    gigantes braised with tomato 109
lime
    ginger and lime daiquiri 24, *26*
    long sparkling ouzo 25, *27*
loukoumades with honey syrup 182
loukanika
    gigantes braised with tomato 109

M
macaroni
    country-style macaroni pie 59
    pastitsio 23
mahlab 213
Mani 129
manouri 193
    chargrilled manouri served with honey-baked peaches *122*, 123
    filo rolls with manouri, walnuts, raisins, figs and mint 180, *181*

marida 21
marouli salad 60, *62*
mastica 213
mayonnaise, lemon 97
meat-stuffed dolmades 88
meatballs *see* keftedes
Mediterranean fish soup 139
Mercouri 187
Messene 157, 168, *168*
Methana Springs 66, *66*
Methoni 160, *160*
meze and ouzo 82–3
mint 214
    feta dip 75, *76*
    filo rolls with manouri, walnuts, raisins, figs and mint 180, *181*
    fried pumpkin balls 130
    meat-stuffed dolmades 88
    ouzo-battered zucchini flowers stuffed with goat's curd 110, *111*
    salt cod fritters with tzatziki 85, 115
    wild greens pie 116, *117*
    zucchini, dill and mint fritters, 80, *81*
myzithra 193
    fried cheese pies 209
Monemvasia 105, 114, *114*
muscatels, cheesecake with 36, *37*

N–O
Nafplio 73, 100
o graten 212
octopus, 30
    baby octopus marinated in honey 31, *84*
    chargrilled octopus 86, *87*
okra ladera 164, 170, *171*
olive oil 164, 213
olive oil cake with spice syrup, walnut, orange and 178
olive oil pastry 209
olives 82, *188*
    country-style macaroni pie 59
    haloumi with fennel, orange and kalamata olives 161
    lamb stuffed with trahanas and wine grapes 197
    olives marinated with lemon and fennel *84*, 188
    salad of black-eyed peas and herbs 144, *145*
    village salad 60, *63*
Olympia 187, 196, *196*
onions 215
orange flower water, poached quinces with 101
oranges
    haloumi with fennel, orange and kalamata olives 161
    snapper with walnut crust and citrus-pomegranate syrup 201
    walnut, orange and olive oil cake with spice syrup 178
oregano 215
ouzo
    braised pork keftedes flavoured with ouzo 28, *29*

Kythirian koumara 119
long sparking ouzo 25, *27*
Mediterranean fish soup 139
meze and 82–3
ouzo-battered zucchini flowers stuffed with goat's curd 110, *111*
ouzo frappé 206, *207*
sea bass with ouzo 49
sparkling watermelon with ouzo foam 25, *26*
under the Hellenic sun 24, *26*

P
Palamidi 98
pasta
    braised veal with orzo *94*, 95
    country-style macaroni pie 59
    pastitsio 23
pastitsio 23
paximadia 213
peach schnapps 24
peaches, chargrilled manouri served with honey-baked *122*, 123
peas 215
pecorino
    capsicums stuffed with cheese 189
    fried cheese pies 209
    ouzo-battered zucchini flowers stuffed with goat's curd 110, *111*
    pastitsio 23
    snapper with walnut crust and citrus-pomegranate syrup 201
    zucchini, dill and mint fritters 80, *81*
Peloponnesian-style roast chicken 142
petimezi 213
pilaf, silverbeet 148
plaki 212
pomegranate syrup, snapper with walnut crust and citrus- 201
pork 213
    braised pork keftedes flavoured with ouzo 28, *29*
    roast pork with lemon potatoes *140*, 141
    souvlaki with skordalia 162, *163*
    stewed pork and tomato with garlic walnut crumb 143
potatoes 215
    braised artichokes 92
    braised green beans and potato *146*, 147
    briam of potato and zucchini 93
    cockerel or chicken in wine with potatoes 169
    fish with olive oil and rigani 79
    roast pork with lemon potatoes *140*, 141
    salt cod fritters with tzatziki 85, 115
    traditional fishermen's soup 136, *137*
prawns
    fried small prawns and baby fish *20*, 21
    prawns and scallops in kataifi with spicy capsicum skordalia *158*, 159
prickly pear 96
psito 212

pulses 213
pumpkin
    fried pumpkin balls 130
    risotto with charred corn, pumpkin, goat's cheese and saffron, *32*, 33

Q–R
quinces with orange flower water, poached 101
rabbit stifado 194, *195*
rabbit with rosemary and garlic in white wine *204*, 205
raisins 213
    filo rolls with manouri, walnuts, raisins, figs and mint 180, *181*
    rocket and raisin salad 35
red eggs 172, 173, *174*
red onions 215
red rock 24, *27*
rice
    Greek creamed rice 153
    meat-stuffed dolmades 88
    risotto with charred corn, pumpkin, goat's cheese and saffron *32*, 33
    silverbeet pilaf 148
ricotta
    country-style macaroni pie 59
    fried cheese pies 209
rigani 213
    bandit's lamb *190*, 191
    braised veal with orzo *94*, 95
    caper dressing 189
    chargrilled octopus 86, *87*
    fish with olive oil and rigani 79
    lamb stuffed with trahanas and wine grapes 197
    Peloponnesian-style roast chicken 142
    slow-roasted lamb ribs with yoghurt and feta sauce 90, *91*
risotto with charred corn, pumpkin, goat's cheese and saffron *32*, 33
rocket
    rocket and raisin salad 35
    wild greens pie 116, *117*
rosemary and garlic in white wine, rabbit with *204*, 205
rozedes 118

S
saffron, risotto with charred corn, pumpkin, goat's cheese and *32*, 33
saganaki 78, 193, 212
salad dressing 98
salads
    black-eyed peas and herbs 144, *145*
    cauliflower 61, *62*
    eggplant *106*, 107
    fennel, artichoke and broad bean *64*, 65
    lentil and chickpea 149
    marouli 60, *62*
    rocket and raisin 35
    salad of beetroot, feta and walnuts 98, *99*
    village 60, *63*

sardines
> Greek 'fish fingers' with lemon mayonnaise 97

sausages
> gigantes braised with tomato 109
> spetzofai 89

scallops in kataifi with spicy capsicum skordalia, prawns and *158, 159*

sea bass filled with ouzo 49

seafood 82
> baby octopus marinated in honey 31, *84*
> barbecued squid filled with spinach and feta *50*, 51
> barbounia wrapped in vine leaves 46, *47*
> chargrilled octopus *86*, 87
> fish with olive oil and rigani 79
> flying squid in garlic and olive oil 67
> fried calamari and artichokes 56, *57*
> fried small prawns and baby fish *20*, 21
> Greek 'fish fingers' with lemon mayonnaise 97
> marinated anchovies 131
> Mediterranean fish soup 139
> prawns and scallops in kataifi with spicy capsicum skordalia *158, 159*
> salt cod fritters with tzatziki *85*, 115
> sea bass with ouzo 49
> snapper with walnut crust and citrus-pomegranate syrup 201
> swordfish souvlaki with capers and dill *198*, 199
> traditional fishermen's soup 136, *137*

selino 215
> braised goat with eggplant 53

semolina
> Kythirian koumara 119
> rozedes 118

sesame bars 125
shallots *see* green onions
sheep's cheese 192, *193*
shellfish *see* prawns
shortbread cookies, Greek *176*, 177
silverbeet 215
> silverbeet pie *44*, 45, *192*
> silverbeet pilaf 148

skordalia
> souvlaki with 162, *163*
> spicy capsicum *158*, 159

snapper
> Mediterranean fish soup 139
> snapper with walnut crust and citrus-pomegranate syrup 201

soup
> Mediterranean fish 139
> traditional fishermen's 136, *137*
> tripe 22

souvlaki with capers and dill, swordfish *198*, 199
souvlaki with skordalia 162, *163*
Sparta 108
spetzofai 89
spice syrup 178
spinach 215
> barbecued squid filled with spinach and feta *50*, 51

chicken stuffed with artichokes, fennel and sundried tomatoes 200
split pea dip 75, *77*
split peas 212

squid 30
> barbecued squid filled with spinach and feta *50*, 51
> flying squid in garlic and olive oil 67
> fried calamari and artichokes 56, *57*

stifado 212
> rabbit 194, *195*

stis skara 212
sto fourno 212
strawberries and toasted almonds, goat's curd with 120, *121*
sultanas 213
sundried tomatoes
> capsicum stuffed with cheese 189
> chicken stuffed with artichokes, fennel and sundried tomatoes 200
> salad of black-eyed peas and herbs 144, *145*

Swiss chard *see* silverbeet
swordfish souvlaki with capers and dill *198*, 199

T

tequila 25
thyme 215
tiganita 212
tis oras 212
tomatoes 82
> braised goat with eggplant 53
> braised green beans and potato *146*, 147
> briam of potato and zucchini 93
> gigantes braised with tomato 109
> Mediterranean fish soup 139
> okra ladera 164, 170, *171*
> rabbit stifado 194, *195*
> spetzofai 89
> stuffed eggplants *112*, 113
> tomato sauce 170
> *see also* sundried tomatoes

trahanas and wine grapes, lamb stuffed with 197
tripe soup 22
Tsakonian 108
tzatziki, salt cod fritters with *85*, 115
tzatziki 74

U–V

under the Hellenic sun 24, *26*
veal with eggplant purée, braised 202, *203*
veal with orzo, braised *94*, 95
vegetables 214
verjuice 213
village salad 60, *63*
vine leaves 215
> barbounia wrapped in vine leaves 46, *47*
> meat-stuffed dolmades 88

vlita 214

vrasto 212

W

walnuts
> chargrilled manouri served with honey-baked peaches *122*, 123
> filo rolls with manouri, walnuts, raisins, figs and mint 180, *181*
> Greek creamed rice 153
> Greek yoghurt and honey 68, *69*
> lamb stuffed with trahanas and wine grapes 197
> salad of beetroot, feta and walnuts 98, *99*
> snapper with walnut crust and citrus-pomegranate syrup 201
> stewed pork and tomato with garlic walnut crumb 143
> walnut, orange and olive oil cake with spice syrup 178

watercress
> wild greens pie 116, *117*

watermelon with ouzo foam, sparkling 25, *27*
whitebait
> fried small prawns and baby fish *20*, 21

wild celery 215
wild greens 48
wild greens pie 116, *117*
wine, 54–5
> blood of Hercules 25, *27*
> cheesecake with muscatels 36, *37*
> cockerel or chicken in wine with potatoes 169
> lamb stuffed with trahanas and wine grapes 197
> rabbit stifado 194, *195*
> rabbit with rosemary and garlic in white wine *204*, 205

wine vinegar 213

Y–Z

yachni 212
yoghurt *see* Greek-style yoghurt
Zorba 138
zucchini 215
> briam of potato and zucchini 93
> zucchini, dill and mint fritters 80, *81*
> zucchini flowers stuffed with goat's curd, ouzo-battered 110, *111*

Zulu bungy 38

Acknowledgements

Any book is the result of a collaboration but this one more than most. First and foremost to my partner in life and love, John Caldon, without whom neither the television series nor book would ever have happened: thank you for your unwavering love, support and faith in both me and Blair. Next thanks go to those who came to my assistance after the tragic loss of Blair: to friend and colleague Jo Anne Calabria who project managed the book; to Peter Forrestal who gave unstintingly of his knowledge and words for the Greek wines spread; to our fabulous Greek researcher and now good friend and colleague, Pamela Garelick, for her advice on recipes, ingredients and all things Greek; to my colleague Ann Kidd, my right hand in all things; to Andrew Ballard who helped test recipes; and to David Humphreys who helped test Blair's cocktails. Without all of you I couldn't have done it.

For bringing it all to fruition my thanks for professionalism and thoughtfulness to Paul McNally and all at Hardie Grant books, to editor Zoë Harpham for her eagle eye, for the wonderful design Emilia Toia (by chance, the cousin of school friends of Blair's), for the gorgeous styling Michelle Noerianto and for the beautiful photography Chris Chen. Last but not least to Lucy Busuttil who cooked the food so well for photography.

Finally to the whole of the SBS team for their friendship and enthusiasm and especially to Erik Dwyer who shaped our show.

An SBS Book
sbs.com.au/food

Published in 2012 by Hardie Grant Books
Hardie Grant Books (Australia)
Ground Floor, Building 1
658 Church Street
Richmond, Victoria 3121
www.hardiegrant.com.au

Hardie Grant Books (UK)
Second Floor, North Suite
Dudley House
Southampton Street
London WC2E 7HF
www.hardiegrant.co.uk

All rights reserved. No part of this publication may be reproduced, stored in a retrieval system or transmitted in any form by any means, electronic, mechanical, photocopying, recording or otherwise, without the prior written permission of the publishers and copyright holders.

The moral right of the author has been asserted.
Copyright text © Lyndey Milan
Copyright food photography © Chris Chen
Copyright location photography © Naked Flame Productions

Cataloguing-in-Publication data is available from the National Library of Australia.
ISBN 978 1 74270 270 4

Publisher: Paul McNally
Project manager and editor: Zoë Harpham
Design manager and illustrations: Heather Menzies
Design and art direction: Emilia Toia
Food photography: Chris Chen
Location photography: Daniel Thomas
Food styling: Michelle Noerianto
Food preparation: Lucy Busuttil
Recipes: Lyndey Milan
Map: Ian Faulkner
Production: Penny Sanderson

Thank you to Robert Gordon Australia for the generous loan of ceramic bowls, plates and homewares and Rust-Oleum for the generous supply of spray paint finishes. Thank you to Earlwood Wines for their assistance in supplying Greek produce.

Colour reproduction by Splitting Image Colour Studio
Printed in China by 1010 Printing International Limited